READING FICTION 1

- Elements of Fiction
- Novels
- Short Stories
- Narrative Poetry

READING in context

READING in context

PRACTICAL READING 1
PRACTICAL READING 2
READING NONFICTION 1
READING NONFICTION 2
READING FICTION 1
READING FICTION 2

SADDLEBACK PUBLISHING·INC.
Three Watson
Irvine, CA 92618-2767

E-Mail: info@sdlback.com
Website: www.sdlback.com

Development and Production: Laurel Associates, Inc.
Cover Design: Elisa Ligon
Interior Illustrations: Ginger Slonaker

ISBN 1-56254-193-5

Printed in the United States of America
05 04 03 02 01   9 8 7 6 5 4 3 2 1

CONTENTS

INTRODUCTION

A NOTE TO THE STUDENT

Skillful readers have many advantages in life. While they are in school, they obviously get better grades. But the benefits go far beyond the classroom. Good readers are also good thinkers, problem-solvers, and decision-makers. They can avoid many of the problems and frustrations that unskilled readers miss out on. In short, good readers have a much greater chance to be happy and successful in all areas of their lives.

READING IN CONTEXT is an all-around skill-building program. Its purpose is to help you achieve your goals in life by making you a better reader. Each of the six worktexts has been designed with your needs and interests in mind. The reading selections are engaging and informative—some lighthearted and humorous, others quite serious and thought-provoking. The follow-up exercises teach the essential skills and concepts that lead to reading mastery.

We suggest that you thumb through the book before you begin work. Read the table of contents. Notice that each of the four units is based on a unifying theme. Then take a moment to look through the four lessons that make up each theme-based unit. Scan one of the *Before reading* paragraphs that introduces a lesson. Glance at the *Preview* and *Review* pages that begin and end each unit. "Surveying" this book (or any book) in this informal way is called *prereading*. It helps you "get a fix on" the task ahead by showing you how the book is organized. Recognizing patterns is an important thinking skill in itself. And in this case it will make you more comfortable and confident as you begin your work.

Happy reading!

PREVIEW

ELEMENTS OF FICTION

LESSON 1: Characters: *Moby Dick*

LESSON 2: Setting: *Dracula*

LESSON 3: Plot: *Dr. Jekyll and Mr. Hyde*

LESSON 4: Dialogue: *The Count of Monte Cristo*

When you complete this unit, you will be able to answer questions like these:

- *In* Dr. Jekyll and Mr. Hyde, *what two forces are in conflict?*

- *In what three ways can dialogue be used to tell a story?*

- *What do we call the character who tells the story in his or her own words?*

- *How important is setting in the novel,* Dracula*?*

PRETEST

Write **T** or **F** to show whether you think each statement is *true* or *false*.

1. _____ *Characters* are the fictional people who play a part in a novel.

2. _____ A novel's *setting* is the sequence of events that make up the story.

3. _____ The words spoken by story characters are called *dialogue*.

4. _____ A novel's *plot* is the time and place the story events take place.

5. _____ The *narrator* of a novel tells the story from his or her own point of view.

6. _____ A story's *plot* always centers on a conflict between opposing characters or forces.

Pretest answers: 1. T 2. F 3. T 4. F 5. T 6. T

CHARACTERS

Before reading . . .

Authors describe their characters in several ways. Sometimes they *directly* describe characters' traits. At other times, they describe *indirectly* through the characters' thoughts, words, and actions. This lesson presents an adapted excerpt from *Moby Dick*, Herman Melville's greatest novel. It is the story of an obsessed man's pursuit of a great white whale. Notice the two ways that Melville describes Captain Ahab. First, Ahab is directly described by Ishmael, the novel's narrator. Then Ahab is described indirectly—through his own words and actions.

MOBY DICK

It was one of those gray and gloomy days. As I mounted to the deck, foreboding shivers ran over me. There on the deck stood Captain Ahab. I saw no sign of bodily illness about him, nor of the recovery from any. His high, broad form seemed to be made of solid bronze. Running down one side of his tawny, scorched face and neck was a long white scar. It resembled the groove in the trunk of a great tree that has been struck by lightning. Had he been born with that mark? Or was the scar left by some wound? No one could say. None of the crew dared to speak of it.

Ahab's grim appearance affected me strongly. At first I hardly noticed its cause—the barbaric white leg upon which he partly stood. I had heard about this ivory leg. Some said it had been fashioned at sea from the polished bone of the sperm whale's jaw. Captain Ahab stood erect, looking straight out at the sea with a fixed and fearless gaze. Not a word did he speak, nor did his officers say anything to him. Moody Ahab stood his ground, in all the dignity of some mighty woe.

* * *

One morning shortly after breakfast, Captain Ahab called the crew to the deck. As the men gathered, all eyes were on Ahab. To the crew, he looked like the weather horizon when a storm is coming up. "You've all heard me give orders about a white whale. Do you see this?" said Ahab, holding up a shiny gold coin. "Whoever spots the whale gets this sixteen-dollar gold piece! Skin your eyes for him, men. Look sharp for white water. If you see but a bubble, sing out!"

"Captain Ahab," said Starbuck, the first mate. "I have heard of a white whale called Moby Dick. But was it not Moby Dick that took off your leg?"

"Who told you that?" cried Ahab. "Aye, Mr. Starbuck, it was Moby Dick that dismasted me. Yes, it was Moby Dick that brought me to this dead stump I stand on now. Aye, aye!" he shouted with a loud, animal sound. It was like the sob of a heart-stricken moose. Then, tossing both arms and cursing, he shouted out again, "Aye! And I'll chase him 'round the Cape of Good Hope, and 'round the Horn. I'll chase him to Norway and beyond to the land of flames before I give him up! And this is what you have shipped for, men! To chase that white whale on both sides of land, and over all sides of earth. There is to be no rest until he spouts black blood and rolls fin over. What say you, men—will you shake hands on it, now? I think you do look brave."

"Aye, aye!" shouted the harpooners and seamen, running closer to the excited old man. "A sharp eye for the white whale! A sharp eye for Moby Dick!" they shouted.

COMPREHENSION

Write your answers on the lines.

1. What causes the "foreboding shivers" the narrator feels as he climbs to the deck of the ship? _____

2. What is the main thing the narrator notices about Captain Ahab's grim appearance? _____

3. According to Ahab, what is to be the crew's main goal?

   _____

4. How far is Ahab prepared to sail in pursuit of the whale?

   _____

5. Why is Captain Ahab so eager to go after the white whale?

   _____

6. What does Ahab plan to do to Moby Dick if and when he catches up with him? _____

7. How does Ahab motivate the crew to search for the whale?

   _____

8. How does the crew respond to Ahab's request for their support?

   _____

CHARACTER STUDY

The following sentences describe characters in the story. Put a checkmark (✔) next to each *true* statement.

1. _____ Captain Ahab seemed to be a pleasant, mild-mannered person.

2. _____ Starbuck, the first mate, liked to argue.

3. _____ Captain Ahab was filled with the desire for revenge.

4. _____ The crew showed a great deal of respect for Captain Ahab.

5. _____ Ahab was in constant fear of the great white whale.

6. _____ The narrator was filled with a sense of foreboding.

POINT OF VIEW

Moby Dick is told from the narrator's (Ishmael's) point of view. How might *Moby Dick* have been different if the story were told from *Captain Ahab*'s point of view? Choose either the first or second paragraphs of the reading. Then rewrite the paragraph from Ahab's point of view. Write on the lines below.

_____

_____

_____

_____

_____

_____

_____

_____

_____

_____

_____

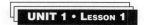

VOCABULARY

Study the **boldface** words from the reading. Then circle a letter to show the correct definition.

1. **foreboding**
   a. fear that something bad is about to happen
   b. fear of missing out on an opportunity
   c. relief at having avoided trouble or danger
   d. expectation of a reward

2. **tawny**
   a. tough, thick
   b. smooth, nearly flawless
   c. brownish orange to light brown
   d. tiny, nearly microscopic

3. **grim**
   a. trim
   b. grimy
   c. gloomy
   d. brief

4. **woe**
   a. wow
   b. worry
   c. sorrow
   d. wonder

5. **dismasted**
   a. broke off a part
   b. distrusted
   c. discovered
   d. disturbed

NOTING DETAILS

Circle a letter to show the correct answer.

1. The narrator compared the scar on Ahab's face and neck to which of the following?
   a. a sperm whale's jaw
   b. the groove in the trunk of a great tree struck by lightning
   c. solid bronze
   d. polished ivory

2. Which word did the narrator use to describe Ahab's white leg?
   a. fixed   b. polished   c. dignified   d. barbaric

3. What did Ahab promise to the crewman who first sighted the white whale?

    a. gold dollar   c. $16.00 gold piece

    b. silver dollar   d. $6.00 gold piece

4. To which of the following did the narrator compare Captain Ahab?

    a. heart-stricken moose   c. sperm whale

    b. white whale   d. Moby Dick

PUZZLER

Two or three words in each sentence are spelled backward. Find and circle these words. Then rewrite the sentences on the lines below, spelling the words correctly. The first one is done for you.

1. As I (detnuom) to the deck, (gnidoberof) shivers ran over me.

   As I mounted to the deck, foreboding shivers ran over me.

2. Moody Ahab stood his dnuorg, in all the ytingid of some ythgim woe.

   _____

   _____

3. He looked like the rehtaew noziroh when a mrots is gnimoc up.

   _____

   _____

4. One morning yltrohs after tsafkaerb, Ahab dellac the crew to the deck.

   _____

   _____

SETTING

Before reading . . .

A story's *setting* is when and where it takes place. In some stories, setting serves mainly as a backdrop for the action. In others, the setting has an important impact on the characters and the events. This adapted excerpt is from the novel *Dracula,* Bram Stoker's famous tale of horror. Notice how the narrator is influenced by the setting.

DRACULA

The driver cracked his whip, called to his horses, and off they swept. As they sank into the darkness, I felt a strange chill, and a lonely feeling came over me. A cloak was thrown over my shoulders, and a rug across my knees. The driver said, "The night is chill, sir, and my master the Count asked me to take good care of you. There is a flask of plum brandy underneath the seat, if you should require it." His words did not reassure me. After a while I struck a match and looked at my watch. It was a few minutes before midnight.

Suddenly a dog howled in a farmhouse far down the road. It was a long, agonized wailing, as if from fear. The sound was taken up by another dog, and then another and another. Soon a wild howling seemed to come from all over the countryside through the gloom of the night. The horses began to strain and rear, but the driver quieted them down. Then, far off in the distance, from the mountains on each side of us, came a louder and sharper howling—that of wolves. Now we could hear the rising wind as well. It moaned and whistled through the rocks that rose on both sides of the road. The branches of the trees crashed together as we swept along.

It grew colder and colder still. Then a fine, powdery snow began to fall. Soon we and all around us were covered with a white blanket.

The baying of the wolves sounded nearer and nearer, as though they were closing around us from every side. I grew dreadfully afraid, and the horses shared my fear. The driver, however, was not in the least disturbed. He kept turning his head left and right, but I could not see anything through the darkness. Just then the moon, sailing through the black clouds, appeared behind the jagged crest of a beetling, pine-clad rock. By its light I saw around us a ring of wolves! I could see their white teeth, lolling red tongues, long sinewy limbs, and shaggy hair. We stopped, and the horses jumped about and reared in terror. The driver got down. I heard his voice raised in a tone of imperious command. Amazingly, the wolves fell back and then back farther still. At last the driver climbed back into the carriage and we were on our way again. Just then a heavy cloud passed across the face of the moon, so that we were again in darkness.

How had the driver caused the wolves to disappear? It seemed so strange and uncanny that a dreadful fear came upon me. I was afraid to speak or move. The journey seemed to last forever. As we swept on our way, we climbed higher and higher into the mountains. We traveled in almost complete darkness, for the rolling clouds obscured the moon. Finally, the driver pulled up the horses in the courtyard of a vast ruined castle. From the tall black windows came no ray of light. The castle's broken battlements showed a jagged line against the moonlit sky. My journey was over. I had arrived at the castle of Count Dracula.

COMPREHENSION

Answer the questions in complete sentences.

1. What effect did the setting have on the narrator? _____

   _____

2. Why did the driver offer the narrator a cloak, a rug, and a

   flask of plum brandy? _____

   _____

3. How were the horses affected by the howling of the dogs?_____

   _____

4. How did the driver make the wolves disappear? _____

   _____

5. How did the narrator respond to the way in which the

   wolves disappeared? _____

   _____

6. How did the narrator keep track of the time in the early

   part of the journey? _____

   _____

7. What was the narrator's final destination? _____

   _____

IDENTIFYING PARTS OF SPEECH

Adjectives are words used to describe a person, place, or thing. Write **A** next to each adjective from the story.

_____ driver	_____ strange	_____ cracked	_____ wild
_____ farmhouse	_____ black	_____ powdery	_____ swept
_____ heavy	_____ dreadful	_____ obscured	_____ broken

ANALYZING MOOD

Vivid details of setting enable writers to create a wide range of moods. A story's mood can have a powerful effect on the characters. In turn, characters can *add* to a story's mood through their behavior, thoughts, and feelings. Circle a letter to answer each question.

1. In the first paragraph, what mood comes over the narrator as he begins his journey?

   a. excitement and impatience
   b. fear and loneliness
   c. warmth and well-being
   d. anger and resentment

2. In the second paragraph, a fearful mood is created by which of the following?

   a. the straining and rearing of the horses
   b. the howling of the dogs and wolves
   c. the way the driver quieted the horses
   d. all of the above

3. In the third paragraph, what causes the narrator to grow "dreadfully afraid"?

   a. the beetling, pine-clad rock
   b. the moon sailing through the black clouds
   c. the baying of the wolves
   d. the horses pulling the carriage

4. In the fourth paragraph, the narrator sees Count Dracula's castle for the first time. Which of the following moods best describes what the narrator is feeling?

   a. cheerfulness   b. fearfulness   c. happiness   d. sadness

NOTING DETAILS

Complete the sentences with the correct details of setting from the story. Put a checkmark (✔) in front of the correct answer.

1. The howling of the dog sounded like agonized

   _____ whining.

   _____ barking.

   _____ yelping.

   _____ wailing.

2. The beetling, pine-clad rock had

   _____ steep sides.

   _____ a jagged crest.

   _____ snow on top.

   _____ hidden crevices.

3. The rising wind moaned and whistled

   _____ in the trees.

   _____ above the castle.

   _____ through the rocks.

   _____ behind the carriage.

4. For much of the trip, the moon was obscured by

   _____ rolling clouds.

   _____ blowing snow.

   _____ tall mountains.

   _____ huge rocks.

VOCABULARY

Choose seven words from the box to correctly complete the sentences.

agonized	**whistled**	**dreadfully**
uncanny	**powdery**	**battlements**
journey	**obscured**	**imperious**

1. The rolling clouds _____ the moon.

2. His voice was raised in a tone of _____ command.

3. The castle's broken _____ showed a jagged line against the moonlit sky.

4. It was a long, _____ wailing, as if from fear.

5. I grew _____ afraid, and the horses shared my fear.

6. The wind moaned and _____ through the rocks.

7. As it grew colder, a fine, _____ snow began to fall.

PUZZLER

Answer each question by filling in the blanks to complete the word from the story. Then unscramble the circled letters to find out what Count Dracula *is*. The first word has been done for you.

1. Which animals jumped about and reared in terror?

    _H_ _O_ (R) _S_ _E_ _S_

2. Who caused the wolves to disappear?

    __ __ __ (__) __ __

3. Which animals surrounded the narrator's carriage?

    __ __ __ __ (__) __

4. What kind of snow began to fall?

    (__) __ __ __ __ __

5. The driver pulled up the horses in which part of the castle?

    __ __ __ __ __ (__) __

6. What did the rolling clouds obscure?

    (__) __ __ __

7. In what kind of vehicle did the narrator travel?

    __ __ __ __ (__) __ __

    Count Dracula is a ___ ___ ___ ___ ___ ___ ___.

PLOT

Before reading . . .

The *plot* is the sequence of events that make up the story. A story's plot always centers on a conflict or struggle between opposing characters or forces. The following adapted excerpt is from Robert Louis Stevenson's novel, *The Strange Case of Dr. Jekyll and Mr. Hyde.* Notice how the characters' actions develop the plot.

DR. JEKYLL AND MR. HYDE

It was late one October night in the city of London. A maid who worked in a house near the river was sitting by her window. She hadn't been able to fall asleep because the moon was very bright. Later, she told what she had seen in the street below her. A tall white-haired gentleman had been walking down the street. Coming toward him was a little man with a strange light step. The two men met just below her window. The tall man, who had a kindly face, stopped to say something to the other man. In the moonlight, she recognized the small man as a certain Mr. Hyde. He had once come to the house of her employer. At the time, she had sensed something evil about him. Almost immediately, she knew that he was a hateful man.

Suddenly, Hyde got very angry and began shouting at the tall man. The older man took a step back, a hurt expression on his face. Then Hyde attacked the man with his heavy walking stick, hitting him again and again! The poor man fell down. But Hyde kept hitting him—and then jumped up and down upon him. Hearing the old man's bones break, the maid passed out. When she came to, she called the police. The old man's body still lay in the street. When the police arrived, they found part of Hyde's walking stick. Hyde had hit the man so hard that he had broken the heavy stick! The killer had not stolen anything from the fallen man. Among the things in his pockets, the police had found a letter addressed to Mr. Utterson, a lawyer.

Early the next morning, the police went to Utterson's house and woke him up. He went with them to where they had taken the body. As soon as he saw the body, Utterson said, "I know this man! I am sorry to say that this is Sir Danvers Carew."

"Good God, sir!" cried the policeman. "An important man! Can it really be?" A sly look came over his face. "This case will make a lot of noise around London," he said. "Perhaps you can help us find the criminal." He then told Utterson what the woman at the window had seen and heard. The lawyer's face grew pale when he heard the name of Mr. Hyde. Then the policeman showed him the broken piece of the walking stick. Utterson didn't want to believe it. Even though it was broken, he recognized the stick. It had been Utterson's gift to a friend many years ago. The friend he had given it to was Dr. Henry Jekyll!

Utterson said nothing about the stick. He only asked the policeman, "Is this Mr. Hyde a small person?"

"The maid said he was quite small—and especially wicked-looking."

Utterson frowned and shook his head. "If you will come with me," he said sadly, "I will take you to his house."

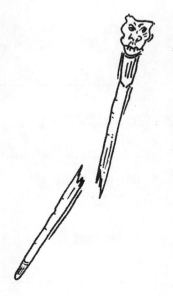

COMPREHENSION

Answer the questions in complete sentences.

1. Why hadn't the maid been able to fall asleep? _____

   _____

2. What did the maid see when she looked out her window? _____

   _____

3. What happened when the two men met just below the

   maid's window? _____

   _____

4. How had the maid reacted to Mr. Hyde the *first* time she had

   seen him? _____

   _____

5. What did the police find when they arrived at the scene of

   the crime? _____

   _____

6. Why did the police go to Mr. Utterson's house? _____

   _____

7. How did the policeman react when he learned the identity

   of the man who had been murdered? _____

   _____

8. What did Utterson offer to do for the police? _____

   _____

PUZZLER

Use the clues to help you complete the crossword puzzle.

ACROSS

3. According to the policeman, the case will make a lot of this.

5. Utterson's profession

8. city where the story takes place

DOWN

1. condition of the stick after the murder

2. month in which the crime takes place

4. type of stick used as the murder weapon

6. who the maid called, after she came to

7. light source that kept the maid from falling asleep

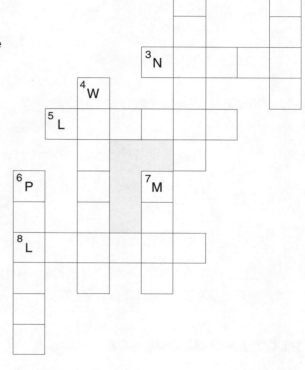

DRAWING CONCLUSIONS

Put a checkmark (✔) next to the best answer to each question.

1. Think about the information given in the story. What conclusion might you draw about the motive for the crime?

   _____ Mr. Hyde knew that Sir Danvers Carew was a wealthy man, and he wanted to steal his money.

   _____ Sir Danvers Carew had gone out of his way to insult Mr. Hyde.

   _____ Robbery was not the motive for the murder.

   _____ Mr. Hyde owed a lot of money to Sir Danvers Carew.

2. Why was Utterson upset when he recognized the broken piece of walking stick?

_____ It meant that there was some connection between his good friend Dr. Jekyll and Mr. Hyde, the murderer.

_____ He hated to see a good walking stick get broken.

_____ It reminded him of a similar walking stick he had once given to his friend.

_____ Walking sticks were not supposed to be used as weapons.

3. Why did Utterson ask the policeman if Mr. Hyde was a small person?

_____ The Mr. Hyde that he knew was a tall person.

_____ He wanted to find out how much the police knew about the case.

_____ He didn't want the police to guess that he knew Mr. Hyde.

_____ He wanted to make sure that the murderer was indeed the Mr. Hyde that he knew.

PLOT AND SEQUENCE

The following story events are out of order. Number the events to show which happened first, second, and so on.

_____ Utterson asked the policeman if Mr. Hyde was a small person.

_____ A tall, white-haired gentleman was walking down the street.

_____ The police found a letter addressed to Mr. Utterson.

_____ Mr. Hyde attacked the man with his heavy walking stick.

_____ A maid had trouble falling asleep because the moon was very bright.

_____ Utterson recognized the broken piece of walking stick.

_____ The maid called the police when she came to.

_____ Early the next morning the police went to Utterson's house.

SYNONYMS

Synonyms are words with the same or nearly the same meaning. Write the synonyms of the following words on the lines. Use words from the story.

1. **toiled** _____
2. **mad** _____
3. **attorney** _____
4. **truly** _____
5. **leaped** _____

6. **detested** _____
7. **robbed** _____
8. **wish** _____
9. **yelling** _____
10. **locate** _____

MAKING PREDICTIONS

The evidence points to some kind of connection between the evil Mr. Hyde and Utterson's friend, Dr. Henry Jekyll. As the plot develops, what relationship between the two men do you think will be revealed? Circle the number before one of the following predictions. Give reasons for your choice on the lines below.

1. Mr. Hyde will turn out to be Dr. Jekyll's brother. Eventually, he will try to murder his own brother in a fit of jealous rage.

2. To Utterson's horror, Dr. Jekyll will turn out to be just as evil as Mr. Hyde. It will be revealed that he has been encouraging Hyde to commit crimes all along.

3. Dr. Jekyll is horrified when he learns of the murder committed by Mr. Hyde. He plans to testify against him at his trial.

4. Utterson is shocked to learn that his friend Dr. Jekyll and the evil Mr. Hyde are actually one and the same person!

_____

_____

_____

_____

DIALOGUE

Before reading . . .

The words spoken by the characters in a novel, short story, or play are called *dialogue*. Dialogue shows what the characters think and feel. Focus on the dialogue in this adapted excerpt from Alexandre Dumas's novel, *The Count of Monte Cristo.* Notice how dialogue tells about the characters, conveys important facts, and develops the plot.

THE COUNT OF MONTE CRISTO

Caderousse, the innkeeper, did not recognize the priest who came in the door.

"Come in. My name is Caderousse," said the innkeeper. "Can I offer you something to eat or drink? Let's go inside." He would never have guessed that the "priest" in front of him was his old neighbor, Edmond Dantes.

When the visitor was seated, he said, "Did you know a sailor named Edmond Dantes?"

"I should say so! Poor Edmond. He was one of my best friends!" said Caderousse. "What has become of him? Is he still living? Is he free? Is he happy?"

"He died a prisoner—sad and without hope," said the priest.

Caderousse's face grew pale. His hand shook as he wiped a tear from his eye. "Poor fellow," he said.

"You seem to have been very fond of the boy," said the priest.

"I was indeed. But at one time I was filled with envy at his happiness," said Caderousse. "Did you know him?"

The priest was looking very closely at Caderousse's face. He said, "I was called to Dantes' bedside while he was dying. He said he never knew why he was in prison. He wished me to clear up the mystery. He said that he had three good friends and a fiancée. One friend was named Caderousse, another Danglars, and the third Fernand. His fiancée was named Mercedes."

"Anyway," said the priest, "Dantes gave me a diamond. He said it had been given to him by another prisoner." The priest took out the diamond, and Caderousse's eyes grew wide.

"Dantes said he wanted to share the diamond with those who once loved him. I was to sell the diamond and divide the money into five parts," said the priest.

"Why *five* parts?" asked Caderousse. "You only named four persons."

"The fifth share was for Dantes' father. But in Marseilles, I heard that he is dead," said the priest.

"Yes, it is only too true," said Caderousse. "The poor man died of sadness, waiting for his son who never returned."

"A sad, sad tragedy," said the priest, trying to hide his tears.

"All the more sad," said Caderousse, "because Dantes' imprisonment was none of God's doing. It was the work of two men who were jealous of him! They are Danglars and Fernand—Dantes' so-called friends! They accused Dantes of working for Napoleon. Danglars wrote the letter the day before the betrothal feast, and Fernand mailed it."

"And you knew all about it, yet you did nothing?" said the priest.

"I wanted to speak out, but Danglars said I would get in trouble," said Caderousse. "Meanwhile, Fernand and Danglars have become happy and rich. Danglars married a rich widow. He now owns a house in Paris, and is known as Baron Danglars. Fernand has become a count. He fought against the Turks in Greece for Ali Pasha. When Ali Pasha died, he left a great fortune to Fernand."

"What about Mercedes?" asked the priest. "I heard she disappeared."

"Disappeared?" said Caderousse. "She is now one of the richest ladies in Paris! When Fernand came back from Greece, he married her. They now have a son, Albert. So you see," said Caderousse, "everything they touched has turned to gold. And everything *I've* done has gone wrong. Only I am poor."

"You are mistaken, my friend," said the priest. "Sooner or later, God remembers us." He gave the diamond to Caderousse. "Take this, it is yours. Dantes had but one true friend," he said. Then the priest said goodbye to Caderousse. He went outside and rode away on his horse.

COMPREHENSION

Answer the questions in complete sentences.

1. Why do you think Edmond Dantes was hiding his true identity?

   _____

2. What did the "priest" say had happened to Dantes? _____

   _____

3. What did Caderousse admit he had once felt toward Dantes?

   _____

4. Why did the priest look closely at Caderousse's face while telling

   him about Dantes' dying words? _____

   _____

5. Why did Caderousse volunteer the information about how

   Fernand and Danglars had betrayed Dantes? _____

   _____

6. What did Caderousse say had happened to Mercedes? _____

   _____

7. What reason did the priest give as to why he was giving

   the diamond to Caderousse? _____

   _____

NOTING DETAILS

The dialogue in the story contains the answers to each of the following questions. Circle the letter of the correct answer.

1. According to the priest, with whom did Dantes say he wanted to share the diamond?

   a. with Fernand and Danglars

   b. with Caderousse, Fernand, and Danglars

   c. with Danglars and Mercedes

   d. with those who had once loved him

2. When did the priest say he had spoken to Dantes?

   a. when Dantes first arrived at the prison

   b. while Dantes was dying

   c. just before Dantes escaped from prison

   d. two months after Dantes' arrival at the prison

3. According to Caderousse, what was the cause of Dantes' father's death?

   a. old age

   b. sadness

   c. heart attack

   d. hunger

4. According to Caderousse, why did Fernand and Danglars betray Dantes?

   a. to earn a reward

   b. to punish him for his crimes

   c. They were jealous of him.

   d. Their families had been longtime enemies.

5. What did Fernand and Danglars accuse Dantes of doing?

   a. stealing from Napoleon

   b. failing to show up at the betrothal feast

   c. stealing from Mercedes

   d. secretly working for Napoleon

CHARACTER TRAITS

Read the lines of dialogue from the story. Then identify who spoke the words and describe the character traits that the dialogue reveals about the speaker. Write your answers on the lines.

1. **"Everything they have touched has turned to gold. And everything I've done has gone wrong. Only I am poor."**

   _____

   _____

2. **"Sooner or later, God remembers us."** _____

   _____

   _____

3. **"I wanted to speak out, but Danglars said I would get in trouble."**

   _____

   _____

DRAWING CONCLUSIONS

Which of the following statements are reasonable conclusions? If you're not sure, think about the information given in the dialogue. Put a checkmark (✔) next to each reasonable conclusion.

1. _____ Danglars and Fernand were not the only ones jealous of Dantes.

2. _____ Caderousse was not especially interested in the diamond.

3. _____ Caderousse realized that the "priest" was really Dantes, but he pretended to be fooled by the disguise.

4. _____ In those days, it was dangerous to work for Napoleon.

5. _____ Edmond Dantes was a good actor.

PUZZLER

First, unscramble the words from the story. Then use the unscrambled words
to complete the lines of dialogue below.

EPRINEKEN

_____

RONESPRI

_____

SPINASHEP

_____

EDIDEBS

_____

MONADID

_____

SUJEOLA

_____

THORTABEL

_____

BREMERMES

_____

ASPIDAPEDER

_____

1. "I was filled with envy at his _____."

2. "The two men were _____ of Dantes."

3. "Dantes said he wanted to share the _____ with
   those who once loved him."

4. "Yes, monsieur. That is my name," said the _____.

5. "Sooner or later, God _____ us."

6. "He said it had been given to him by another _____."

7. "What about Mercedes?" he asked. "I heard she has
   _____."

8. "Danglars wrote the letter the day before the _____
   feast."

9. "I was called to Dantes' _____ while he was dying."

Unit 1 ══════════ **REVIEW** ══════════════

INTERPRETING DIALOGUE

The following questions all refer to the excerpts from stories in lessons 1–4.
Circle a letter to show the correct answer to each question.

1. **What did Captain Ahab mean when he said, "It was Moby Dick that dismasted me"?**

   a. Moby Dick had rammed the whaling vessel, knocking down its main mast.

   b. Moby Dick had escaped from the whale hunters, thereby making fools of them.

   c. Moby Dick had caused Captain Ahab to lose a leg.

   d. Moby Dick had beaten Captain Ahab in a race across the ocean.

2. **What did the London policeman mean when he said to Mr. Utterson, "This case will make a lot of noise around London"?**

   a. Detectives would be knocking on doors all around town, trying to get information about the murder.

   b. The crime would draw widespread attention, because the victim was a well-known citizen of London.

   c. Angry protests over the murder would erupt throughout London.

   d. Policemen all over London would be rounding up suspects who fit the description of the murderer.

3. **Why did Caderousse say that Dantes' imprisonment was "the work of two so-called friends, Danglars and Fernand"?**

   a. He wanted the diamond for himself.

   b. He was eager to share the diamond.

   c. He knew the priest wouldn't tell on him.

   d. Danglars and Fernand were really innocent.

4. **What did Dantes, disguised as a priest, mean when he said, "Sooner or later, God remembers us"?**

   a. God remembers all our deeds, the good as well as the bad.

   b. Eventually God rewards us for our good deeds.

   c. It doesn't pay to be greedy.

   d. As far as God is concerned, friendship means a lot.

NOVELS

When you complete this unit, you will be able to answer questions like these:

- *Why might a young character and an older character have different viewpoints about war?*

- *How does an author reveal the thoughts and feelings of a character who doesn't speak?*

- *How does the time a story takes place affect the characters' dialogue?*

- *How could details of setting make a life-or-death difference to a character in a story?*

PRETEST

Write **T** or **F** to show whether you think each statement is *true* or *false*.

1. _____ Descriptions of the plants and animals in a certain place are details of plot.

2. _____ Characters are described by their thoughts as well as their actions.

3. _____ Story events are always told from the main character's point of view.

4. _____ Characters' dialogue can give the reader important hints about how the plot will develop.

5. _____ The words spoken by a character directly mirror his or her feelings.

6. _____ A story's setting has little influence on characters' feelings.

Pretest answers: 1. F 2. T 3. F 4. T 5. F 6. F

CHARACTERS' VIEWPOINTS

Before reading . . .

The Red Badge of Courage, by Stephen Crane, is a novel about the Civil War. It tells about the experiences of Henry, a young man from the North who joins the Union army. In this adapted excerpt, the reader learns about Henry and his mother. As you read, think about the difference between two characters' viewpoints. Notice how these differences are revealed by their thoughts, words, and actions.

THE RED BADGE OF COURAGE

Henry had dreamed of battles all his life. The great bloody wars of storybooks and his imagination had thrilled him with their sweep and fire. In his daydreams, Henry had always fought the battles as a mighty hero. But Henry didn't really believe that such battles were possible anymore. They belonged in the distant past, along with heavy crowns and high castles.

When Henry had first heard about the war in his own country, he thought it must be some sort of a play affair. He knew that men dressed in military uniforms. But he was sure they would never use the guns they carried. Men today were too timid for war. Everything had changed. Religion and education, he felt, had long since gotten rid of the killer instinct in men.

But the more news Henry heard about the war, the more eager he became to enlist. It seemed that this war was not a game. Real battles *were* being fought, and Henry longed to see it all for himself.

Henry's mother was dead set against his enlisting. She gave him hundreds of reasons to stay home on the farm rather than go off to the field of battle. But almost every day the newspapers gave accounts of great victories. The village gossip was filled with tales of glory. Before long, Henry made up his mind. He said to his mother, "Ma, I'm going to enlist."

"Henry, don't you be a fool," his mother had replied.

But Henry went to the village and enlisted in a regiment that was being formed there. When he got home, his mother was milking the cow. "Ma, I've enlisted," he said.

There was a short silence. Finally, Henry's mother said, "The Lord's will be done, Henry." Then she continued to milk the cow.

Soon the day came for Henry to leave. He got dressed in his new blue uniform. It was time to say goodbye to his mother. She was busy peeling potatoes. When she looked up at Henry, he could see two tears rolling down her cheeks.

"You watch out, Henry," she said. "Don't think you can lick the whole Rebel army at the start—because you can't. You're just one little fellow among a whole lot of others. You've got to keep quiet and do what they tell you. Avoid the company of bad men who will try to get you to drink and to swear. Don't ever do anything you would be ashamed of. If you ever have to risk your life, or take another man's life, just think about what's right. The Lord will take care of us all."

Then they said goodbye, and Henry walked toward the gate. He looked back once. His mother was kneeling among the potato peels. She was looking up, her face stained with tears, her thin body shaking. Suddenly Henry felt ashamed of himself, but he bowed his head and kept going.

COMPREHENSION

Answer the questions in complete sentences.

1. What had Henry dreamed about all his life? _____

   _____

2. At first, why did Henry think the war in his own country was

   just a "play affair"? _____

   _____

3. According to Henry, what two things were responsible for stamping

   out the killer instinct in men? _____

   _____

4. Why do you think Henry's mother was against his enlisting?

   _____

5. Why did Henry finally decide to enlist in the army? _____

   _____

6. How did Henry's mother react to the news of his enlisting?

   _____

7. At the end of the passage, why did Henry feel ashamed?

   _____

CHARACTER STUDY

The following sentences describe character traits. Put a checkmark (✔) next to each statement that is *true*.

1. _____ Henry had a vivid imagination.

2. _____ Henry's mother was a selfish woman.

3. _____ Henry was a lazy young man.

4. _____ Henry's mother loved her son very much.

5. _____ Henry didn't care what his mother thought.

6. _____ Henry's mother hated farm work.

7. _____ Henry was looking for adventure and excitement.

SYNONYMS

Synonyms are words that have the same or nearly the same meaning. Read each **boldface** word from the story. Then circle its synonym.

1.	**thrilled**	fulfilled	excited	chilled	threatened
2.	**timid**	brave	troubled	afraid	careless
3.	**enlist**	join	write	count	include

ANTONYMS

Antonyms are words that have opposite meanings. Circle the antonym of each **boldface** word from the story.

1.	**hero**	giant	winner	coward	fighter
2.	**war**	battle	peace	fight	army
3.	**ashamed**	proud	sorry	glad	suspicious

PUZZLER

First, unscramble the words from the story. Then use the unscrambled words to complete the sentences below.

MYADDSERA   ITYLARIM   TILENS

_____   _____   _____

SPANERSWEP   GELAVIL   INUMORF

_____   _____   _____

NEKLIGEN   EDAMASH   SPOGIS

_____   _____   _____

1. Men at war dressed in _____ uniforms.

2. In his _____, Henry always fought heroic battles.

3. After seeing his mother's tears, Henry felt _____.

4. Henry went to the _____ to enlist in the army.

5. Henry's mother was _____ among the potato peels.

6. The village _____ was filled with tales of glory.

7. Henry got dressed in his new blue _____.

8. Henry was eager to _____ in the army.

9. Almost every day the _____ told of great victories.

MAKING PREDICTIONS

In his imagination, Henry has bravely taken part in many battles. What do you think will happen when Henry is in a real battle, fighting against a real enemy? Circle the number of one of the following answers. Then give reasons for your choice on the lines below.

1. Henry will fight bravely and prove to be a hero.

2. Henry will prove to be a coward and run away in the middle of a battle.

3. Because he won't follow orders, Henry will get into trouble.

_____

_____

_____

_____

_____

SEQUENCE OF EVENTS

Number the story events to show which happened first, second, and so on.

_____ Henry got dressed in his new blue uniform.

_____ Henry's mother was dead set against his enlisting.

_____ Henry said goodbye and walked toward the gate.

_____ Henry's mother continued to milk the cow.

_____ Henry thought the war was just some sort of play affair.

_____ Suddenly, Henry felt ashamed of himself.

_____ Henry went to the village and enlisted in the army.

_____ The gossip in the village was filled with tales of glory.

SETTING

Before reading . . .

Daniel Defoe wrote his famous novel, *Robinson Crusoe,* in 1720. It tells the story of a young Englishman who finds himself stranded on a small island in the middle of nowhere. In this adapted excerpt, Robinson Crusoe begins to explore his new surroundings. As you read, notice how Crusoe uses the details of the setting to survive.

ROBINSON CRUSOE

When the storm was over, I stepped outside of my tent. Once again, the weather was fine. There was not even a single cloud in the sky. I climbed all the way to the top of my hill and looked out in every direction.

Now I knew for sure that I was on an island. I could see some rocks and two smaller islands to the west. But in every other direction there was nothing but the sea. And I could see no signs of any other people on the island. There were no houses, roads, or even trails. So I now had to accept that I was all alone.

Whether I lived or died would be completely up to me. Was I clever enough to survive by myself? I would soon find out. When I got back to my camp, I was hungry. I picked up one of the guns and went looking for game.

As I came to the edge of a wooded area, I saw a large bird sitting on a tree. I aimed my gun and fired. There was a sudden explosion of wild screeches as a great many birds flew up out of the trees. None of the birds looked familiar to me. But the one I aimed at had fallen to the ground. It looked like some type of hawk. Unfortunately, its flesh was not fit to eat.

Later I walked into the woods, hoping to find food that would be more suitable, perhaps some sort of fowl. Before long, I found the type of bird I was looking for. I shot two plump fowls that were somewhat like ducks. I brought them back to my camp, and found them very good to eat.

Protecting myself from dangerous beasts or men was one of my main concerns. I decided to set up my camp quickly so that I would be as safe as possible. As much as I could, I wanted to turn my camp into a fortress. After giving it some thought, I came up with a plan.

There was a wide crack in the rock wall behind my tent. I thought that I might be able to dig into the crack and create a storage space. By removing a good deal of earth and rocks from the crack, I made myself a cave. This turned out to be a safe, dry place to keep my things. In fact, it served as my cellar. It also turned out to be a good place to build a fire during rainy weather.

The other part of my plan was to build a wooden fence. I first drew a half-circle around my camp. In this half-circle I placed two rows of strong stakes. I drove them deep into the ground until they stood very firm. The stakes were about five and a half feet tall. I carefully placed two long rows of stakes about six inches apart.

It took me a long time—almost a year—to complete the fence. Cutting the stakes, bringing them to my camp, and driving them into the ground was hard work. The complete process took three days for each stake. I did not build a door in the fence as an entrance to my fortress. Instead, I used a short ladder to go over the top. Once inside, I lifted the ladder over the fence after me. Inside, I felt completely safe.

COMPREHENSION

Write **T** or **F** to show whether each statement is *true* or *false*.

1. _____ Robinson Crusoe himself would be responsible for his own survival.

2. _____ After seeing no signs of other people, Robinson Crusoe was still not sure whether or not he was alone on the island.

3. _____ The first bird Robinson Crusoe shot looked like some sort of hawk.

4. _____ One of Robinson Crusoe's main concerns was protecting himself from dangerous beasts or men.

5. _____ The stakes in the fence were about seven feet tall.

6. _____ Robinson Crusoe built a door in the fence as an entrance to his fortress.

7. _____ Robinson Crusoe felt completely safe inside his fortress.

VOCABULARY

Many words have more than one meaning. The correct meaning of a word depends on how the word is used in context. Put a checkmark (✔) next to the correct meaning of each **boldface** word as it is used in the story.

1. **game**   _____ activity engaged in for amusement

       _____ wild animals hunted for sport or food

2. **direction**   _____ line along which something is pointing or facing

       _____ instruction or order

3. **stakes**   _____ prizes in a contest

       _____ pointed pieces of wood driven into the ground

4. **drove**   _____ operated a vehicle

       _____ forced by pressing or digging

40

DETAILS OF SETTING

Some details of the setting helped Robinson Crusoe survive on the island. In what way was each of the following details of setting important? Write your answers on the lines.

1. the hill near Robinson Crusoe's tent _____

_____

_____

2. the fowl in the woods _____

_____

_____

3. the wide crack in the rock wall behind the tent _____

_____

_____

IDENTIFYING PARTS OF SPEECH

A *noun* is used to name a person, place, or thing. A *verb* is used to describe an action or state of being. Read the following words from the story. Then write **N** if the word is a *noun* or **V** if the word is a *verb*.

_____ storm	_____ stepped	_____ tent	_____ climbed
_____ knew	_____ survive	_____ explosion	_____ aimed
_____ hawk	_____ fortress	_____ decided	_____ men
_____ removing	_____ cellar	_____ ground	_____ fence
_____ process	_____ lifted	_____ build	_____ ladder

POINT OF VIEW

Robinson Crusoe is written in the "first person." This means that everything is told from Robinson Crusoe's point of view. What we read are *his* thoughts and feelings about living alone on the island. Now imagine how *you* would feel if you were all alone on that island. Answer the following questions from your *own* point of view.

1. What type of shelter would you build for yourself in order to feel safe on the island?

    _____

    _____

    _____

2. Since nobody knows where you are, you may not be rescued for a long time—if ever. What are your thoughts about the possibility of never seeing your friends or family again?

    _____

    _____

    _____

3. What people, belongings, or activities would you miss the most?

    _____

    _____

    _____

4. Think about the types of food you might eat on the island. How would you find animals to hunt? Which vegetables and fruits would you try to grow? How would you design a garden?

    _____

    _____

    _____

PUZZLER

Use the clues to help you complete the crossword puzzle. Answers are words from the story.

ACROSS

3. appropriate; meets a particular need

4. structure used for climbing up or down

6. previously known

8. continuous series of actions or operations

DOWN

1. storage space beneath a house; basement

2. building designed to protect those inside against an attack

5. natural underground chamber with an opening to the surface

7. bird, such as a chicken or duck

MAKING PREDICTIONS

What do you think is going to happen to Robinson Crusoe? Will he ever be rescued? Will he have to spend the rest of his life alone on the island? How would you like the story to end? Write your answer on the lines below. If you need more space, use another sheet of paper.

_____

_____

_____

_____

_____

CHARACTERS' THOUGHTS

Before reading . . .

The Call of the Wild, Jack London's memorable novel, takes place during the time of the Alaska gold rush. This adapted excerpt introduces Buck, the main character, who happens to be a dog. As you read, notice the different ways London uses to show what Buck is thinking and feeling.

THE CALL OF THE WILD

Buck did not read the newspapers. If he did, he would have found out that trouble was coming. Not just for himself, but for every dog with strong muscles, from Puget Sound to San Diego. This was because, in the Arctic darkness, a precious yellow metal—gold—had been found. Thousands of men were rushing north to the frozen Northland. These men needed dogs— heavy dogs with strong muscles and furry coats. Big dogs would be able to work hard. And their furry coats would protect them from the cold.

Buck lived on a large estate in the sunny Santa Clara Valley. Judge Miller's place, it was called. Buck ruled over this great estate. Here he was born. Here he had lived all four years of his life. There were other dogs here—but these little dogs did not count. They came and went. Many of them lived in the kennels. Some lived in hidden corners of the house.

But Buck was neither house dog nor kennel dog. The whole place was his, and he roamed wherever he pleased. He went swimming and hunting with the Judge's sons. He went on walks with the Judge's daughters, and he played with the Judge's grandsons. On winter nights he would lie at the Judge's feet by the fire in the library.

Buck's father was Elmo, a huge St. Bernard. His mother, Shep, had been a Scotch shepherd dog. Buck took great pride in himself and carried himself like a king. Outdoor activity had kept down the fat and hardened his muscles.

This was the kind of dog Buck was in the fall of 1897. But because Buck did not read the newspapers, he did not know that gold had been discovered in the Klondike. And he did not know that one man at Judge Miller's place was about to change his life forever. Manuel, one of the gardener's helpers, loved to gamble. And in order to gamble, he always needed more money.

One night the Judge was at a meeting of the Raisin Growers' Association. The boys were busy planning a sports event. No one saw Manuel lead Buck off through the orchard. Buck thought they were just out for an evening walk. No one saw them arrive at the little train station known as College Park— nobody except the man who was waiting there for them. When this man talked with Manuel, money passed between them.

"You might wrap up the goods before you deliver them," the stranger said gruffly.

Manuel doubled a piece of thick rope under the collar around Buck's neck. "Twist it, and you'll choke him plenty," said Manuel.

Buck had accepted the rope with quiet dignity. He had learned to trust people he knew. He gave them credit for a wisdom beyond his own. But when the ends of the rope were placed in the stranger's hands, Buck growled. He did this to show the men he didn't like what was happening. His pride led him to think that this was all he needed to do. Once the men saw he wasn't happy, they would remove the rope.

But to Buck's surprise the rope tightened around his neck, shutting off his breath. In quick rage he sprang at the stranger. But the man was ready for him. He grabbed Buck by the throat. Then, with a twist, he threw him over on his back. Then the rope grew even tighter. Buck struggled in a fury, his tongue hanging out of his mouth, his big chest heaving. Never in his life had he been so badly treated! And never had he been so *angry*. But as the rope tightened, his strength slowly left him. Soon his eyes glazed over. He knew nothing when the train stopped, and the two men threw him into the baggage car.

COMPREHENSION

Answer the questions in complete sentences.

1. Why were thousands of men rushing north? _____

   _____

2. What kind of trouble would Buck soon have to face? _____

   _____

3. How was Buck's life different from that of the other dogs on

   Judge Miller's estate? _____

   _____

4. Who was Manuel, and why did he need more money? _____

   _____

5. Why had Buck allowed Manuel to place a rope around his neck?

   _____

6. Why did Buck growl when the ends of the rope were placed in

   the stranger's hands? _____

   _____

DRAWING CONCLUSIONS

Based on the information given in the story, which of the following statements are reasonable conclusions? Put a checkmark (✔) next to each sensible conclusion.

1. _____ Buck led a happy life on Judge Miller's estate.

2. _____ Buck was afraid of the other dogs on the estate.

3. _____ Buck was not very smart, since he should have known not to trust Manuel.

4. _____ Although the stranger's treatment of Buck was cruel, the man most likely loved dogs.

5. _____ Buck was devoted to the members of the Miller family.

6. _____ The men rushing to the frozen Northland were hoping to strike it rich.

PUZZLER

Complete the words from the story that answer the questions. Then unscramble the circled letters to learn why Buck was needed in the Northland. The first one has been done for you.

1. What was Buck's mother's name?

S H (E) P

2. What type of shepherd was Buck's mother?

(_) _ _ _ _ _

3. Trouble was coming to dogs from Puget Sound to where?

_ _ _ (_) _ _ _

4. In addition to swimming, what did Buck do with the Judge's sons?

_ _ _ _ _ _ _ (_)

5. What was the name of Buck's father?

_ (_) _ _

6. The gold-seekers were going in which direction?

_ (_) _ _ _ _

7. Where was gold discovered in 1897?

_ _ _ _ (_) _ _ _

In the Northland, Buck was needed

as a _ _ _ _   _ _ _.

47

VOCABULARY

Check the correct definition of each **boldface** word from the story.

1. **precious**
   a. _____ having an attractive appearance
   b. _____ of great value or high price
   c. _____ of interest to only a few people
   d. _____ prone to accidents

2. **estate**
   a. _____ particular mood or state of mind
   b. _____ geographical section of a country
   c. _____ parcel of land with a large house on it
   d. _____ important business plan

3. **kennel**
   a. _____ shelter for dogs or cats
   b. _____ fish-processing plant
   c. _____ manufacturer of dog food
   d. _____ training program for veterinarians

4. **orchard**
   a. _____ open, grassy area or field
   b. _____ area with groves of fruit trees
   c. _____ thicket of trees and bushes
   d. _____ colorful flower garden

IDENTIFYING DETAILS

Authors include details in their writing to help clarify or explain their ideas. Some details tell *where, when,* or *how* something happened. Others tell *who* or *what* was involved. Write your answers on the lines.

1. Where was Judge Miller's estate located? _____

2. In what year was gold discovered in the Klondike? _____

3. What kind of dog was Buck's mother? _____

4. What kind of dog was Buck's father? _____

5. Who brought Buck to the train station? _____

6. What was the name of the train station? _____

7. What did the two men do to Buck when the train stopped? _____

_____

CAUSE AND EFFECT

Read each pair of sentences. Decide which is a *cause* and which is an *effect*.
Write **C** next to the *cause* and **E** next to the *effect*.

1. _____ Buck did not read newspapers.

   _____ Buck had no idea that trouble was coming.

2. _____ Men were rushing to the frozen Northland.

   _____ In 1897, gold was discovered in the Klondike.

3. _____ Manuel needed more money to gamble.

   _____ Manuel kidnapped Buck and sold him to a stranger.

4. _____ Buck allowed a rope to be placed around his neck.

   _____ Buck had learned to trust people he knew.

DIALOGUE

Before reading . . .

Nathaniel Hawthorne's novel, *The Scarlet Letter,* was published in 1850. It is a gripping tale of secret sin and ruthless revenge in the 17th century. In this adapted excerpt, Hester Prynne is being punished by the Puritans of Boston. For her crime—refusing to name the father of her baby—she is made to stand on a scaffold. Suddenly she sees a familiar face in the crowd. As you read, notice how important details are revealed through the characters' dialogue.

THE SCARLET LETTER

As Hester stood holding her child on the scaffold, she wished that she could be somewhere else. To keep her mind off her suffering, she looked out over the crowd. On its outer edge, two men caught her eye—an Indian and the white man standing beside him. The white man was dressed in a strange combination of English and Indian clothes.

Hester stared at the white man's face. He had an intelligent expression, as though he had spent many years studying books. Then Hester noticed that one of his shoulders rose higher than the other. Suddenly she realized that she knew this man. Her eyes met his across the crowd. But as soon as the man saw that Hester recognized him, he put his finger to his lips.

Then the man touched the shoulder of a townsman standing next to him. "Sir, who is that woman?" he asked. "Why is she set up to public shame?"

The townsman said, "Friend, you must be a stranger in this region. Otherwise you would have heard of Mistress Hester Prynne and her evil ways. She has raised a great scandal in Master Dimmesdale's church."

"I am indeed a stranger in these parts. I have met with misfortune on sea and on land," said the stranger. "For a long time I was held captive by the Indians south of here. This Indian with me brought me here to arrange for my ransom. Will you tell me of Hester Prynne's— am I saying her name correctly?—of this woman's crimes? What has brought her to this scaffold?"

"Truly, I will tell you, friend," said the townsman. "How glad your heart must be to find yourself here in Boston—where sin is punished. This woman was the wife of an English gentleman. He had decided to come over and join us in Massachusetts. He sent his wife here before him, staying behind to look after some business. But sir, would you believe it . . . In the two years she has been here, no word has come of her husband! And the foolish young wife, being left here alone. . . ."

"Aha! I see," said the stranger with a bitter smile. "A wise husband might have known what would happen. So who is the baby's father?"

"In truth, friend, that remains a mystery," answered the townsman. "Mistress Prynne refuses to name him."

"The husband should come himself to look into this mystery," said the stranger in a harsh, stern voice.

"He should, indeed—if he is still alive," said the townsman. "Most likely, he is at the bottom of the sea. That is why our good judges have not sentenced her to death. They have ordered that she stand on the scaffold for three hours. Also, she must wear the scarlet letter for the rest of her life."

"A wise sentence," said the stranger, bowing his head. "Something bothers me, however. Surely her partner in sin should at least stand on the scaffold by her side. Surely he will be known. He will be known! *He will be known!*"

The stranger bowed politely to the townsman. Then he and the Indian made their way through the crowd. All this time, Hester had not taken her eyes off the stranger. Now she was almost glad that she was in front of a large crowd. It would have been worse, much worse, to greet this man—her husband—face to face, the two of them alone.

COMPREHENSION

Answer the questions in complete sentences.

1. What physical characteristic of the strange white man caused Hester to suddenly recognize him? _____

   _____

2. According to the stranger, why did the Indian take him to Boston?

   _____

3. For what crime or sin was Hester being punished? _____

   _____

4. According to the townsman, what remained a mystery? _____

   _____

5. According to the stranger, what should Hester's husband do?

   _____

6. According to the townsman, what had probably happened to Hester's husband? _____

   _____

7. Why was Hester almost glad she was standing on the scaffold?

   _____

IDENTIFYING DIALOGUE

Read the following lines of dialogue. Write **T** if the *townsman* is the speaker.
Write **S** if the *stranger* is the speaker.

1. _____ "Sir, who is that woman?"

2. _____ "She has raised a great scandal in Master Dimmesdale's church."

3. _____ "For a long time I was held captive by the Indians south of here."

4. _____ "A wise husband might have known what would happen."

5. _____ "The husband should come himself to look into this mystery."

6. _____ "Surely he will be known. He will be known! *He will be known!*"

INTERPRETING DIALOGUE

Circle the letter next to the best answer to each of the following questions.

1. The stranger asked why Hester was **"set up to public shame."** What was he referring to?

   a. Hester had to stand on the scaffold before a crowd of people.

   b. Hester had to beg the townspeople for forgiveness.

   c. Hester had to tell all about the sins she had committed.

2. The townsman referred to **"Mistress Hester Prynne and her evil ways."** What did he mean?

   a. Hester was known for never telling the truth.

   b. Hester, a married woman, had committed a sin by having a baby with another man.

   c. Hester had the habit of stealing from people.

3. The stranger said, **"A wise husband might have known what would happen."** What did he mean?

   a. Hester would make plans to return to England.

   b. Hester could only be expected to live alone for a certain period of time. Then she would become involved with another man.

   c. Hester would begin divorce proceedings after a while.

4. The townsman said, **"That is why our good judges have not sentenced her to death."** What did he mean?

   a. The judges believed that Hester's husband was probably dead.

   b. The judges wanted Hester to live and suffer for a long time.

   c. The judges were sympathetic to Hester's problems.

5. The stranger said, **"Something bothers me, however."** What was he referring to?

    a. He felt bad that Hester had to stand on the scaffold.

    b. He felt that Hester's partner in sin should stand on the scaffold at Hester's side.

    c. He wanted to help Hester get off the scaffold.

NOTING DETAILS

Check the words that correctly complete each sentence.

1. Hester was told to stand on the scaffold for

    _____ 24 hours.

    _____ 12 hours.

    _____ three hours.

    _____ three days.

2. The stranger had been held captive by the Indians

    _____ north of Boston.

    _____ west of Boston.

    _____ far from Boston.

    _____ south of Boston.

3. Hester had raised a great scandal

    _____ in Dimmesdale's church.

    _____ at an Indian village.

    _____ in the local school.

    _____ on the scaffold.

4. Hester had not heard from her husband for

    _____ six months.

    _____ 12 months.

    _____ two years.

    _____ six years.

VOCABULARY

Put a checkmark (✔) next to the definition of each word from the story.

1. **scandal**   a. _____ a shoe consisting of a sole strapped to the foot

             b. _____ circumstance or action that offends an established code of behavior

2. **scarlet**   a. _____ bright red   b. _____ shameful

3. **scaffold**   a. _____ a platform on which a criminal is punished   b. _____ a folding ladder

SENTENCE COMPLETION

Fill in the missing words to complete the following sentences from the story.

1. To keep her mind off her suffering, Hester looked out _____
   _____.

2. Then Hester noticed that one of his shoulders _____
   _____.

3. All this time, Hester had not taken her eyes _____
   _____.

4. The stranger bowed politely _____.

PUZZLER

First, unscramble the words from the story. Then use the words to complete the
sentences. Finally, unscramble the circled letters to learn who the stranger is.

FLADCOF(S)	**(S)HREDLOSU**	**EZECRO(D)ING**
_____	_____	_____
FRIN(U)TOMES	**SE(B)USI(N)S**	**CRES(T)(A)L**
_____	_____	_____

1. One of the man's _____ rose higher than the other.

2. The man saw that Hester _____ him.

3. The stranger had met with _____.

4. Hester had to stand with her child on a _____.

5. Hester had to wear a _____ letter the rest of her life.

6. Hester's husband stayed behind to look after _____.

   The stranger is Hester's __ __ __ __ __ __ __.

55

IDENTIFYING CHARACTERS

The characters presented in this unit are the people (or animals) about whom the novel is written. Draw a line from the novel on the left to the appropriate character or characters on the right. (Note: You may connect more than one character to the same novel.)

1. *Robinson Crusoe*

2. *The Red Badge of Courage*

3. *The Scarlet Letter*

4. *The Call of the Wild*

Judge Miller

Buck

Manuel

Henry

Robinson Crusoe

the townsman

Hester Prynne

Henry's mother

NOTING DETAILS

Circle a letter to show the correct answer to each question.

1. Where did Buck spend the first four years of his life?

   a. the Klondike

   b. Santa Clara Valley

   c. an island

   d. the frozen Northland

2. Which was the most important item that Robinson Crusoe needed to find in order to survive on the island?

   a. a house to live in

   b. an animal to keep as a pet

   c. food and fresh water

   d. a rowboat

3. What did Henry's mother tell him to avoid?

   a. missing too many meals

   b. disobeying an officer

   c. the company of bad men

   d. being captured

SHORT STORIES

LESSON 1: Irony: *The Story of an Hour*

LESSON 2: Reflection: *The Peasant Marey*

LESSON 3: Surprise Ending: *The Gift of the Magi*

LESSON 4: Cause and Effect: *The Necklace*

When you complete this unit, you will be able to answer questions like these:

■ *How can a story character's memory from the past affect events in the present?*

■ *How does a character's social class affect his or her attitudes?*

■ *Is the willingness to sacrifice as valuable as the sacrifice itself?*

■ *In what ways can a character's vanity affect a story's plot development?*

PRETEST

Write **T** or **F** to show whether you think each statement is *true* or *false*.

1. _____ If the reader pays close attention to plot developments, there is no such thing as a surprise ending.

2. _____ One character can have two very different feelings about the same event.

3. _____ Short stories usually have fewer characters than novels do.

4. _____ Confined in a prison setting, all characters react in much the same way.

5. _____ A character's generosity is directly related to the amount of money he or she has.

6. _____ The consequences of a mistaken idea can sometimes be felt for many years.

Pretest answers: 1. F 2. T 3. T 4. F 5. F 6. T

IRONY

Before reading . . .

Kate Chopin's famous short story, "The Story of an Hour," tells about a married woman who longs for freedom and independence. As you read the adapted story, notice how the woman is affected by a piece of news. How does her reaction change when she learns that the news was false?

THE STORY OF AN HOUR

Everyone knew that Mrs. Mallard had heart trouble. So they tried to be as gentle as possible in telling her the news of her husband's death. It was her sister Josephine who told her. Her husband's friend Richards was also there. He had been in the newspaper office when news of the train accident was received. Brently Mallard's name was first on the list of the "killed."

Mrs. Mallard did not try to deny the news as many women have done. She cried at once, suddenly and wildly, in her sister's arms. Then, when the storm of grief was over, she went to her room alone. She would allow no one to follow her. She sank into a big comfortable armchair in front of the open window. Except when a sob rushed up her throat, she was quite still. From the window she could see the leafy tops of trees. Countless birds were chirping.

As Mrs. Mallard looked out at the patches of blue sky between the clouds, she started thinking. Slowly an overwhelming feeling crept over her. It was a feeling of joy! Under her breath she said, "Free, free, free!" Her eyes were bright and her heart was beating fast. She tried to beat back the feeling. She knew she would cry again when she saw his kind, tender hands folded in death. But she could also see past that sad moment—to a long parade of years that would belong to her alone. She would live for herself. No longer would there be a strong will bending hers and trying to control her.

And yet she had felt love for him—sometimes. Often she had not. Yet, what did it matter! Love seemed as nothing compared to the new freedom she felt! She now saw this as the strongest feeling she had ever had! *Free! Body and soul free!*" she kept whispering to herself.

Josephine was kneeling outside the closed door, asking to come in. "Louise, what are you doing? You'll make yourself ill. Open the door!"

"Go away. I am not making myself ill," said Mrs. Mallard. No, she was drinking in life itself, through that open window. She imagined all the days ahead of her that would be her own. She was still a young woman with a pretty face. She prayed that her life would be long. Yet only yesterday, she had thought how terrible it would be if life were too long! Finally, she stood up and let her sister in. She put her arm around Josephine's waist, and they walked down the stairs. Richards stood waiting for them.

Someone was opening the front door with a key. It was Brently Mallard who walked in, carrying his suitcase and umbrella. He was a little worn out from taking the later train. He had not been near the scene of the accident. He did not even know there had been one. At the sound of Josephine's loud scream, he stood amazed. Richards quickly tried to move in front of Brently so that his wife would not see him. But Richards was too late.

When the doctors came, they said she had died of heart disease—of the joy that kills.

COMPREHENSION

Circle the letter of the best answer to each question.

1. Why did Josephine and Richards take care to break the bad news as gently as possible to Mrs. Mallard?

    a. They knew Mrs. Mallard hated to hear bad news.

    b. They knew Mrs. Mallard had heart trouble.

    c. They hated to speak of sad things.

    d. They weren't certain their information was accurate.

2. Upon first hearing the news, how did Mrs. Mallard react?

    a. She felt a strong sense of relief.

    b. She didn't show any emotion.

    c. She cried suddenly and wildly.

    d. She went to her room alone.

3. When she was alone in her room, what kind of feeling crept over Mrs. Mallard?

    a. anger   b. fear   c. sadness   d. joy

4. What did Mrs. Mallard now see as the strongest feeling she had ever had?

    a. freedom   b. love   c. loyalty   d. devotion

5. Why did Richards try to prevent Mrs. Mallard from seeing her husband?

    a. He was embarrassed that the news of Brently's death was false.

    b. Suddenly seeing her husband might be too much of a shock for her weak heart.

    c. He was in shock at seeing Brently and wasn't thinking clearly.

    d. He knew she was glad to be free of her husband.

DRAWING CONCLUSIONS

Put a checkmark (✔) beside the best answer to each question.

1. What conclusion might you draw about Mrs. Mallard's views about her marriage?

   _____ She believed that true happiness can only come through marriage.

   _____ She believed that if a woman loses her husband, it is best to get married again as soon as possible.

   _____ She believed that marriage is more advantageous for a woman than for a man.

   _____ She believed that it is better to be single and independent, rather than married and under a husband's control.

2. What conclusion could be drawn about Mrs. Mallard's feelings toward her husband?

   _____ She felt she didn't know him.

   _____ She loved her husband with all her heart.

   _____ She resented him more than she loved him.

   _____ She had never loved her husband.

3. What conclusion might you draw as to the reason for Mrs. Mallard's death?

   _____ Her weak heart could not handle so much sudden happiness.

   _____ Her weak heart could not handle the sudden loss of the freedom for which she had been longing.

   _____ Because of her weak heart, she would have died even if her husband had not shown up.

   _____ The sight of her husband had nothing whatever to do with her death.

PLOT AND SEQUENCE

Number the story events to show which happened first, second, and so on.

_____ Mrs. Mallard put her arm around her sister's waist, and they walked down the stairs.

_____ Mrs. Mallard looked out at the patches of blue sky and started thinking.

_____ Brently Mallard walked in, carrying his suitcase and umbrella.

_____ Mrs. Mallard sank into a big armchair in front of the open window.

_____ Mrs. Mallard prayed that her life would be long.

_____ Richards tried to shield Brently from his wife's view.

_____ Josephine told Mrs. Mallard the bad news.

_____ The doctors said Mrs. Mallard had died of heart disease—of the joy that kills.

VOCABULARY

Choose six words from the box to complete the sentences.

armchair	**parade**	**freedom**	**accident**	**umbrella**
kneeling	**newspaper**	**control**	**imagined**	**countless**

1. Mrs. Mallard _____ that all the days ahead of her would be her own.

2. Josephine was _____ outside the closed door.

3. Love seemed as nothing compared to the new _____ she felt.

4. Brently Mallard walked in, carrying his suitcase and _____.

5. Richards had been in the _____ office when news of the train accident was received.

6. No longer would her husband's strong will bend hers and try to _____ her.

7. She saw past that sad moment to a long _____ of years that would belong to her alone.

8. She sank into a comfortable _____ in front of the open window.

PUZZLER

Use the clues to help you complete the crossword puzzle with words from the story. All of the answers are *adjectives,* words that describe a person, place, or thing.

ACROSS

4. Mrs. Mallard sank into a ___ armchair.

6. She was still a young woman with a ___ face.

7. Someone was opening the ___ door with a key.

DOWN

1. ___ birds were chirping.

2. Mrs. Mallard now saw this as the ___ feeling she ever had.

3. She would cry again when she saw his kind, ___ hands.

5. She was drinking in life itself through that ___ window.

63

REFLECTION

Before reading . . .

This lesson presents "The Peasant Marey," a short story written by the great 19th-century Russian novelist Fyodor Dostoevsky. The main character is an unnamed prisoner in Siberia who is greatly moved by a memory from his past. Study the main character as you read the adapted excerpt from the story. How do his memories help him survive the harsh conditions of life in prison?

THE PEASANT MAREY

It was Easter Monday. The air was warm and the sky blue, but I was plunged in gloom. I wandered around the prison yard, counting the bars in the strong iron fence. It was a prison "holiday," a day when the convicts didn't have to work. Since the guards left them alone, many of the prisoners got drunk. Some were singing crude songs. Some began fighting with each other. All of this made me sick. I could never bear the wild parties of the common people. Here in prison it was even worse than in the world outside.

I walked by the Polish prisoner Miretski. Like me, he was imprisoned not for a crime, but for political reasons. "I hate these outlaws!" he hissed at me in a low voice. Walking back to my cell, I passed six convicts who were beating a huge man called Gazin. They beat him until the big man was lying on the ground—out cold. The six men had come close to killing him.

In my cell, I lay down in my bunk. I closed my eyes and put my hands behind my head. I liked to rest that way. No one bothered a sleeping man. It gave me time to dream and think. After a while I was able to forget my surroundings. Soon I became lost in memories. During my four years in prison, I was always thinking about my past.

This day, I remembered a time when I was nine years old. I was walking through the countryside on a sunny August afternoon. As I entered the nearby woods, I heard someone call out, "Wolf! Wolf!" Screaming, I rushed out to the clearing. I ran straight toward a peasant who was plowing the land. It was our peasant Marey. He was a tall man, about 50 years old. He had a large, dark brown beard. "There's a wolf there!" I cried.

"There are no wolves around here," Marey said. "You've been dreaming, my boy." He looked at me with a worried smile. "Don't be frightened. Oh, you poor thing, you! There, there." He was trying to calm me down. Finally, I realized that there was no wolf. I had imagined the shout.

"Well, I'll go now," I said, feeling a little ashamed of myself.

"Run along, son. I'll be watching you," he said. "Don't you worry about a thing. Everything's all right."

While I made my way home, Marey stood by his horse and watched me. He nodded his head and smiled tenderly every time I looked around. Soon I forgot all about Marey. As a serf, he was the property of my family. I was the son of his master. Yet, this coarse and ignorant Russian peasant had reached out to me. He could not have looked at me with brighter love had I been his own son.

When my mind returned to the present, my feelings about the other convicts had changed. All hatred and anger had left my heart. I walked around the prison, looking into the faces I met. That evening I met Miretski again. He could have no memories of Marey or peasants like him. Prison was much harder for Miretski than for me!

COMPREHENSION

Circle the letter of the best answer to each question.

1. Which of the following did **not** happen during the prison "holiday"?

   a. Prisoners got drunk.

   b. The guards watched the prisoners closely.

   c. Prisoners fought with each other.

   d. Prisoners sang crude songs and told cruel jokes.

2. Why had the narrator and Miretski been sent to prison?

   a. They had been convicted of murder.

   b. They had been convicted of robbery.

   c. They were political prisoners.

   d. They had been convicted of smuggling.

3. Which of the following was **not** a reason why the narrator liked to lie down in his bunk, close his eyes, and put his hands behind his head?

   a. No one bothered a sleeping man.

   b. It gave him time to dream and think.

   c. He was able to forget his surroundings.

   d. It gave him time to think about the other prisoners.

4. Why did the boy scream and rush out of the woods?

   a. He thought he saw a wolf.

   b. He thought someone called out, "Wolf! Wolf!"

   c. He heard wolves howling.

   d. He was afraid he would get lost.

5. How did Marey react when the boy told him about the wolf?

   a. He tried to calm the boy down.

   b. He said it was good that the boy had run from the woods.

   c. He said the woods were full of wolves.

   d. He made fun of the frightened boy.

6. How did the narrator's feelings toward the other convicts change?

    a. He hated them as much as ever.

    b. He had even less patience for their ignorance.

    c. He no longer hated them.

    d. He wanted to befriend all of them.

VOCABULARY

Read the **boldface** words from the story. Then put a checkmark (✔) beside the definition that matches the way the word is used in the story.

1. **gloom**

    a. _____ confusion

    b. _____ sorrow

    c. _____ silence

    d. _____ terror

3. **convicts**

    a. _____ guards

    b. _____ criminals

    c. _____ prisoners

    d. _____ conscripts

2. **crude**

    a. _____ cunning

    b. _____ cruel

    c. _____ vulgar

    d. _____ strange

4. **peasant**

    a. _____ a kind of pheasant

    b. _____ one who plows the soil for a wealthy landowner

    c. _____ one who lives in the country

    d. _____ professional gardener

DIALOGUE

Authors often use dialogue to reveal what a character is feeling. First, read the lines of dialogue from the story. Then identify the speaker. Finally, circle the letter that best expresses what the character is feeling.

1. "I hate these outlaws!" _____

    a. pleasure   b. surprise   c. excitement   d. hatred

2. "There's a wolf there!" _____

    a. sadness   b. happiness   c. fear   d. sorrow

3. "Don't be frightened. Oh, you
   poor thing, you! There, there." _____

   a. spite   b. compassion   c. disgust   d. fear

4. "Well, I'll go now." _____

   a. anger   b. shame   c. excitement   d. guilt

ANTONYMS

Antonyms are words with opposite meanings. In each group, circle the antonym of the **boldface** word from the story.

1. **plunged**   sunk   emerged   jumped   leaped

2. **common**   ordinary   typical   usual   unusual

3. **frightened**   scared   fearful   unafraid   terrorized

4. **ashamed**   sorry   proud   mortified   embarrassed

5. **ignorant**   educated   uneducated   clueless   uninformed

6. **brighter**   lighter   shinier   darker   whiter

DRAWING CONCLUSIONS

Which of the following statements are reasonable conclusions, based on the information given in the story? Put a checkmark (✔) beside each reasonable conclusion.

1. _____ The narrator hated the Polish prisoner Miretski.

2. _____ The narrator's family were wealthy landowners.

3. _____ The narrator was offended by the crude behavior of the other prisoners.

4. _____ The narrator would have been happy to live as a peasant.

5. _____ The narrator's memories of Marey gave him a new appreciation for his fellow prisoners, whom he had previously hated.

PUZZLER

First, unscramble the words from the story. Then use the unscrambled words to complete the sentences below.

LILACOPIT	GINGINS	GRINSORUSUND
_____	_____	_____
RENSORISP	**UDICOSENTRY**	**RIMOSEME**
_____	_____	_____

1. I was walking through the _____ on a sunny afternoon.

2. Many of the _____ got drunk on holidays.

3. After a while, I was able to forget my _____.

4. Some prisoners were _____ crude songs.

5. Like me, Miretski was in prison for _____ reasons.

6. Soon I became lost in my _____ of the past.

SURPRISE ENDING

Before reading . . .

This lesson presents an adapted excerpt from O. Henry's famous short story, "The Gift of the Magi." As the story opens, a woman agonizes over not having enough money to buy a nice Christmas gift for her husband. The story has a surprise ending. As you read, try to predict how the story will end.

THE GIFT OF THE MAGI

One dollar and 87 cents. Della began to cry. Tomorrow would be Christmas day, and she had only $1.87. Was it enough to buy her husband Jim a present? She had been saving every penny she could for months, with this result. Twenty dollars a week doesn't go far. Expenses had been greater than she had calculated.

Suddenly, she whirled from the window. She had an idea as she stood before the mirror. She pulled down her hair and let it fall to its full length. It reached below her knees. There were two possessions in which Della and Jim took a mighty pride. One was Jim's gold watch that had been his father's and his grandfather's. The other was Della's hair. Now it fell about her, rippling and shining like a cascade of brown waters. Quickly and nervously, Della pinned up her hair again while a tear or two splashed on the worn red carpet.

Della put on her old brown jacket and went outside. She stopped in front of a sign that read: *Mme. Sofronie. Hair Goods of All Kinds*. She went up the flight of stairs to the shop. "Will you buy my hair?" asked Della.

When Madame Sofronie saw Della's beautiful brown hair, she offered $20.00 for it.

"Give it to me quick," said Della. She then spent the next two hours ransacking the stores for Jim's present. At last she found it—a platinum chain for Jim's watch. She paid $21.00 and hurried home with 87 cents and the watch chain. When she got home, she got out curling irons and tried to repair the damage to her hair. Then she heard Jim's footsteps on the stairs. "Please God," she thought, "make him think I am still pretty."

When Jim saw Della, he stared at her with a peculiar expression on his face. "Jim, darling," cried Della. "Don't look at me that way. I had my hair cut off and sold so that I could buy you a nice Christmas gift."

"You've cut off your hair?" asked Jim, as if he could not believe it. He drew a package from his overcoat pocket and threw it upon the table. "When you open the package, you may see why you had me going at first."

Della tore open the package and burst into tears. Inside the package was a set of beautiful tortoiseshell combs. For a long time Della had admired them in a Broadway shop window. Now they were hers—but her hair was gone! "My hair grows fast, Jim!" she cried as she ran to get his present. She held it out to him upon her open palm. "Isn't it a dandy, Jim? Give me your watch. I want to see how it looks on it."

Instead of obeying, Jim tumbled down on the couch. He put his hands under the back of his head and smiled. "Della," he said, "let's put our Christmas presents away and keep them a while. They're too nice to use just now. I sold the watch to get the money to buy your combs. And now, let's have dinner."

The magi were wise men who brought gifts to the Babe in the manger. They invented the art of giving Christmas presents. But of all who give gifts, these two young people were the wisest. They are the magi.

COMPREHENSION

Write **T** or **F** to show whether each statement is *true* or *false*.

1. _____ Della had not been able to save enough money to buy a Christmas present for her husband.

2. _____ The only thing that Della and Jim took pride in was Jim's gold watch.

3. _____ Madame Sofronie was not interested in Della's hair.

4. _____ Della had admired the tortoiseshell combs for a long time.

5. _____ Jim did not want the platinum watch chain.

6. _____ Jim had sold his watch to get money to buy the combs.

7. _____ The author compared Della and Jim to the magi.

VOCABULARY

Choose six words from the box to complete the sentences.

calculated	**cascade**	**ransacking**	**magi**	**tortoise**
platinum	**manger**	**possessions**	**curling**	**peculiar**

1. Della's hair fell like a _____ of brown water.

2. Della used a _____ iron to repair the damage to her hair.

3. Jim bought Della combs made out of _____shell.

4. Expenses had been greater than Della had _____.

5. Della spent two hours _____ the stores for Jim's present.

6. Jim stared at Della with a _____ expression.

CHARACTER STUDY

Put a checkmark (✔) next to each *true* statement about a character's traits.

1. _____ Della loved her husband very much.

2. _____ Jim was not a very generous person.

3. _____ Della did not think Christmas day was very important.

4. _____ Jim was not especially fond of Della's long hair.

5. _____ Della wanted to look pretty in her husband's eyes.

6. _____ According to the author, Jim and Della were not the wisest of gift givers.

7. _____ Gifts meant a lot to Della and Jim.

SEQUENCE OF EVENTS

Number the events from the story to show which happened first, second, and so on.

_____ Della put on her old brown jacket and went outside.

_____ Della whirled from the window.

_____ Jim tumbled down on the couch and put his hands behind his head.

_____ Della sold her long brown hair to Madame Sofronie.

_____ Della spent two hours ransacking the stores for Jim's present.

_____ Della ran to show Jim his present.

_____ Jim stared at Della with a peculiar expression on his face.

_____ Della bought Jim a watch chain for $21.00.

IDENTIFYING PARTS OF SPEECH

Nouns are words that name a person, place, or thing. *Verbs* are words that describe an action or state of being. Read the following words from the story. Write **N** if the word is a *noun* or **V** if the word is a *verb*.

_____ calculated   _____ window   _____ penny   _____ pulled

_____ dollars   _____ whirled   _____ expenses   _____ hair

_____ jacket   _____ walking   _____ looked   _____ footsteps

_____ found   _____ ransacking   _____ offered   _____ expression

_____ admired   _____ overcoat   _____ hurried   _____ invented

NOTING DETAILS

Put a checkmark (✔) in front of the detail that correctly completes each sentence.

1. Della wanted to buy Jim a gift, but she had only

   _____ $1.78.

   _____ 87 cents.

   _____ $1.87.

   _____ $20.00.

2. Madame Sofronie bought Della's hair for

   _____ $12.00.

   _____ $20.00.

   _____ $2.00.

   _____ $200.00.

3. For _____, Della ransacked the stores in search of a gift.

   _____ 12 hours

   _____ 20 hours

   _____ two hours

   _____ two days

4. Jim bought Della a set of combs made out of

   _____ turtle shell.

   _____ tortoise hair.

   _____ tortoiseshell.

   _____ tortoise skin.

PUZZLER

Fill in the blanks with the words from the story that answer the questions. Then unscramble the circled letters to learn what Madame Sofronie gave to Della. The first word has been completed for you.

1. What was the watch chain that Della bought made of?

   P L A T I N (U) M

2. What color was Della's old jacket?

   _ (_) _ _ _

3. What had Della been doing with her pennies?

   _ _ _ (_) _ _

4. What kind of expression did Jim have on his face?

   _ _ (_) _ _ _ _ _

5. What did Della have to climb to get to Madame Sofronie's shop?

   _ (_) _ _ _ _

6. Jim's watch had belonged to his father and to whom else?

   _ _ (_) _ _ _ _ (_) _ _

What did Madame Sofronie give to Della?

_ _ _ _ _ _

SYNONYMS

Synonyms are words that have the same or nearly the same meaning. Write a synonym for each of the following words from the story.

1. rapidly _____

2. repair _____

3. hurried _____

4. under _____

5. cascade _____

6. peculiar _____

7. tumbled _____

8. wise _____

CAUSE AND EFFECT

Before reading . . .

This lesson presents an adapted excerpt from "The Necklace," a story by Guy de Maupassant. The main character is Mathilde Loisel, a woman who borrows a necklace from a friend. As you read, think about the importance of cause and effect in the development of the plot.

THE NECKLACE

Mathilde Loisel was one of those pretty and charming girls of a certain type. It was as if, by a mistake of destiny, she had been born into a family of clerks. There was no possibility of her marrying a rich man. So she married a clerk who worked at the Ministry of Public Instruction. But Mathilde was always unhappy. She felt that she deserved a better life. Although she had a servant to do the housework, she owned no fine dresses, no jewels— nothing grand. And she loved nothing but fine things; she felt *made* for that. She wanted only to please, to be envied, to be charming, to be sought after. She had a rich friend, Madame Forestier, who was a former schoolmate. But Mathilde no longer liked to visit her. Each time she came home, she suffered from envy.

One day, Mathilde's husband had some news. They had been invited to a ball at the palace of the Ministry. Mathilde burst into tears. "I have no dress!" she cried. "I can't go to such a ball." So her husband gave her 400 francs to buy a suitable dress. But even when she bought a fine dress, Mathilde was sad. Her husband asked her what was wrong. "It annoys me not to have a single piece of jewelry to wear," she said. "There's nothing more humiliating than to look poor among other women who are rich. I'd almost rather not go at all." Her husband then suggested that she borrow some jewelry from her friend, Madame Forestier.

The next day, Mathilde went to her friend. Madame Forestier brought out her jewelry and told Mathilde to choose something. She chose a superb necklace of diamonds. At the ball, Mathilde was the prettiest woman of all. She was elegant, gracious, smiling, and crazy with joy. All the men looked at her, asked her name, and wanted to waltz with her. The Loisels didn't leave the ball until about 4:00 in the morning. When they got home, Mathilde wanted to take one last look at herself in the mirror. Suddenly she uttered a cry. The necklace was no longer around her neck! Her frantic husband went out to search for it. On foot he retraced their route home from the ball. But he found nothing.

The next day, Loisel went to the police and to the cab companies. Then he went to the newspaper offices to offer a reward. But the necklace did not turn up. So they went from jeweler to jeweler, searching for a necklace that looked like the one that was lost. Finally, they found one. The jeweler agreed to sell it to them for 36,000 francs. Loisel had 18,000 francs which his father had left him. He would borrow the rest. They bought the necklace, and Mathilde returned it to her friend. Now the dreadful debt had to be paid. Mathilde and her husband moved to a cheaper apartment. She did all the heavy housework their servant used to do. Her husband worked nights as well as days.

At the end of 10 years, they had paid back everything. Mathilde looked old now. One Sunday she ran into Madame Forestier, who still looked young and beautiful. Mathilde decided to tell her the truth about the necklace. At first her friend didn't recognize her. Then she said, "Oh, poor dear, how you have changed!"

Mathilde told her how she had lost the necklace and bought another just like it. "We have spent ten years paying for it," she said.

"You say you bought a necklace of *diamonds* to replace mine?" said Madame Forestier.

"Yes. You never noticed it, then! They were very alike."

Madame Forestier, strongly moved, took her two hands. "Oh, my poor Mathilde! Why, my necklace was paste. It was worth at most 500 francs!"

COMPREHENSION

Answer the questions in complete sentences.

1. Why was Mathilde always unhappy? _____

   _____

2. Why didn't Mathilde like to visit her friend, Madame Forestier?

   _____

3. According to Mathilde, what was the most humiliating thing of all?

   _____

4. Where did Mathilde's husband search for the necklace? _____

   _____

5. How did Mathilde's life change after her husband bought

   the replacement necklace? _____

   _____

6. Why didn't Madame Forestier recognize Mathilde at first? _____

   _____

VOCABULARY

Look in the story for each of the following words. Use context clues to help
you decide what each word means. Then write the meanings on the lines.
Use a dictionary if you need help.

1. **destiny** _____

2. **suitable** _____

3. **francs** _____

4. **humiliating** _____

5. **paste** _____

DIALOGUE

Dialogue often reveals what a character is feeling at a particular moment. First, identify the speaker of each line of dialogue. Then circle the letter that best expresses what the character is feeling.

1. "Oh, poor dear, how you have changed!" _____

    a. pleasure   b. surprise   c. joy   d. anger

2. "Therefore, I can't go to this ball." _____

    a. happiness   b. pride   c. sadness   d. worry

3. "I'd almost rather not go at all." _____

    a. anger   b. annoyance   c. shock   d. spite

4. "Oh, my poor Mathilde!" _____

    a. joy   b. pleasure   c. anger   d. pity

CAUSE AND EFFECT

Read each pair of sentences. Write **C** if the sentence names a *cause*. Write **E** if it names an *effect*.

1. _____ Loisel gave Mathilde 400 francs to buy a dress.

    _____ Mathilde had no dress to wear to the ball.

2. _____ Mathilde felt that she deserved a better life.

    _____ Mathilde was always unhappy.

3. _____ Mathilde had no jewelry to wear to the ball.

   _____ Mathilde borrowed a necklace from Madame Forestier.

4. _____ The necklace was no longer around Mathilde's neck.

   _____ Mathilde uttered a cry when she looked in the mirror.

5. _____ Mathilde's husband bought a replacement necklace.

   _____ Madame Forestier's necklace was lost.

NOTING DETAILS

Some details in the story tell *where, when,* or *how* something happened. Others tell *who* or *what* was involved. Use details from the story to answer the questions.

1. Where did Mathilde's husband work? _____

2. What kind of necklace did Mathilde's
   husband buy?   _____

3. How much did the necklace cost? _____

4. How long did it take Mathilde and her husband
   to pay back the money they had borrowed? _____

5. How much did Madame Forestier
   say her necklace was worth? _____

DRAWING CONCLUSIONS

Based on the information given in the story, which of the following statements are reasonable conclusions? Put a checkmark (✔) next to each sensible conclusion.

1. _____ Mathilde was unhappy because she was not rich.

2. _____ Loisel was not a good husband.

3. _____ Madame Forestier felt that she was better than other people.

4. _____ Mathilde was very concerned about what other people thought of her.

5. _____ The replacement necklace cost more than the Loisels could afford.

6. _____ Mathilde must have been shocked to learn that the stones in Madame Forestier's necklace were not real diamonds.

PUZZLER

First, unscramble the words from the story. Then use the unscrambled words to correctly complete the sentences below.

CHATOMOSEL

_____

SEEDVERD

_____

ISOPILBISTY

_____

WEJYREL

_____

TRUDEET

_____

TENTRAPAM

_____

1. Mathilde was annoyed that she didn't have any _____.

2. Mathilde _____ a cry when she looked in the mirror.

3. Mathilde and her husband moved to a cheaper _____.

4. She had a rich friend who was a former _____.

5. There was no _____ of Mathilde marrying a rich man.

6. Mathilde felt that she _____ a better life.

──── REVIEW ────

IDENTIFYING STORY ELEMENTS

Circle the letter of the correct answer to each question.

1. Which story does **not** have a surprise ending?
   a. "The Necklace"
   b. "The Gift of the Magi"
   c. "The Story of an Hour"
   d. "The Peasant Marey"

2. In which story does a woman react to bad news in a surprising way?
   a. "The Story of an Hour"
   b. "The Peasant Marey"
   c. "The Necklace"
   d. "The Gift of the Magi"

3. Which story is **not** about a husband and wife?
   a. "The Necklace"
   b. "The Gift of the Magi"
   c. "The Peasant Marey"
   d. "The Story of an Hour"

4. In which story is a man's view of his fellow prisoners changed by a memory from his childhood?
   a. "The Story of an Hour"
   b. "The Gift of the Magi"
   c. "The Peasant Marey"
   d. "The Necklace"

CAUSE AND EFFECT

Name the *cause* of the events described below. Look back at the stories if you need help. Write your answers on the lines.

1. What caused an unnamed political prisoner to have a new appreciation of his fellow prisoners?

   _____

2. What caused Mathilde and her husband to buy an expensive diamond necklace?

   _____

3. Why did Mrs. Mallard's reaction to the news of her husband's death change from grief to relief?

   _____

4. What caused Della to sell her beautiful long hair?

   _____

PREVIEW

NARRATIVE POETRY

Lesson 1: Timelessness: *Casey at the Bat*

Lesson 2: Rhyme Scheme: *Paul Revere's Ride*

Lesson 3: Point of View: *The Rime of the Ancient Mariner*

Lesson 4: Repetition: *The Charge of the Light Brigade*

When you complete this unit, you will be able to answer questions like these:

- *What adjective is used to describe a poem that tells a story?*

- *In poetry, what is the repetition of the same beginning sound called?*

- *How does a poet create* rhythm *in a poem?*

- *How might a poem written 100 years ago be different from a poem today?*

PRETEST

Write **T** or **F** to show whether you think each statement is *true* or *false*.

1. _____ Paul Revere is a famous hero of America's Civil War.

2. _____ To ancient seamen, the albatross was a symbol of good luck.

3. _____ Baseball has been played in America for only about 75 years.

4. _____ Poets sometimes repeat certain phrases or lines to heighten the dramatic effect.

5. _____ The bravery of men at war is not a fit subject for poetry.

6. _____ Paul Revere's famous ride took place in the state of Massachusetts.

Pretest answers: 1. F 2. T 3. F 4. T 5. F 6. T

TIMELESSNESS

Before reading . . .

Some stories never grow old. Ernest Lawrence Thayer wrote the following poem in 1888—well over 100 years ago. Yet the dramatic event he describes is truly timeless. As you read, notice the many similarities between today's baseball fans and the crowd in the stands at Mudville.

CASEY AT THE BAT

1   The outlook wasn't brilliant for the Mudville nine that day.
The score stood four to two, with but one inning more to play,
And then when Cooney died at first, and Barrows did the same,
A pall-like silence fell upon the patrons of the game.

2   A straggling few got up to go in deep despair. The rest
Clung to the hope which springs eternal in the human breast;
They thought, "If only Casey could but get a whack at that—
We'd put up even money now, with Casey at the bat."

3   But Flynn preceded Casey, as did also Jimmy Blake,
And the former was a hoodoo, while the latter was a cake;
So upon the stricken multitude grim melancholy sat,
For there seemed but little chance of Casey getting to the bat.

4   But Flynn let drive a single, to the wonderment of all,
And Blake, the much despised, tore the cover off the ball;
And when the dust had lifted, and men saw what had occurred,
There was Jimmy safe at second and Flynn a-hugging third.

5   Then from five thousand throats and more there rose a lusty yell;
It rumbled through the valley, it rattled in the dell;
It pounded on the mountain and recoiled upon the flat,
For Casey, mighty Casey, was advancing to the bat.

6   There was ease in Casey's manner as he stepped into his place;
There was pride in Casey's bearing and a smile lit Casey's face.
And when, responding to the cheers, he lightly doffed his hat,
No stranger in the crowd could doubt 'twas Casey at the bat.

7   Ten thousand eyes were on him as he rubbed his hands with dirt;
Five thousand tongues applauded when he wiped them on his shirt.
Then while the writhing pitcher ground the ball into his hip,
Defiance flashed in Casey's eye, a sneer curled Casey's lip.

8 And now the leather-covered sphere came hurtling through the air,
And Casey stood a-watching it in haughty grandeur there.
Close by the sturdy batsman the ball unheeded sped—
"That ain't my style," said Casey. "Strike one!" the umpire said.

9 From the benches, black with people, there went up a muffled roar,
Like the beating of the storm-waves on a stern and distant shore;
"Kill him! Kill the umpire!" shouted someone on the stand;
And it's likely they'd have killed him had not Casey raised his hand.

10 With a smile of Christan charity great Casey's visage shone;
He stilled the rising tumult; he bade the game go on;
He signaled to the pitcher, and once more the dun sphere flew;
But Casey still ignored it, and the umpire said, "Strike two!"

11 "Fraud!" cried the maddened thousands, and echo answered "Fraud!"
But one scornful look from Casey and the audience was awed.
They saw his face grow stern and cold, they saw his muscles strain,
And they knew that Casey wouldn't let that ball go by again.

12 The sneer has fled from Casey's lip, his teeth are clenched in hate;
He pounds with cruel violence his bat upon the plate.
And now the pitcher holds the ball, and now he lets it go,
And now the air is shattered by the force of Casey's blow.

13 Oh, somewhere in this favored land the sun is shining bright;
The band is playing somewhere, and somewhere hearts are light.
And somewhere men are laughing, and little children shout;
But there is no joy in Mudville—mighty Casey has struck out.

COMPREHENSION

Write your answers on the lines.

1. Which two players batted first and second in the last inning
of the game? _____

2. Why did the crowd think there was "little chance" that Casey
would come up to bat? _____

_____

3. Why did Casey "doff" his hat to the crowd? _____

_____

4. How many people were in the
   stands watching the game? _____

5. Why did someone in the crowd yell, "Kill the umpire!"? _____

_____

6. How is the description of Casey's face in verse 12 different
   from the description in verse 7? _____

_____

7. What did Casey do before he swung at the last pitch? _____

_____

8. What would the final score have been if Casey had hit a home run?

_____

VOCABULARY

Choose six words from the box to complete the sentences. Use a dictionary if
you need help.

rhythm	poetic	verse	poem	sonnet
composition	rhyme	novelist	poet	stanza

1. A _____ is an imaginative piece of writing that
   has a regular pattern of sounds.

2. The group of lines that make up one section of a poem is called
   a *verse* or a _____.

3. The flowing pattern of sounds, accents, or beats in a poem is
   called _____.

4. The writer of a poem is called a _____.

5. A _____ is a song or poem that tells a story
   in short verses.

6. Words that _____ have the same ending sounds.

RHYMING

Write three words of your own that *rhyme* with each word from the poem.

1. **fell** _____ _____ _____

2. **hope** _____ _____ _____

3. **grim** _____ _____ _____

4. **dust** _____ _____ _____

5. **rose** _____ _____ _____

6. **ease** _____ _____ _____

SYNONYMS

Synonyms are words with the same or nearly the same meaning. Write
the words in the poem that are **synonyms** of the words in *italics*.

1. In verse 1, which word means
   customers?   _____

2. In verse 3, which word means
   came before or *ahead of*?   _____

3. In verse 3, which word means
   a *large crowd*?   _____

4. In verse 5, which word means
   loud, spirited, and *energetic*?   _____

5. In verse 6, which word means *removed* and *tipped*?

   _____

6. In verse 8, which word means *disregarded* or *ignored*?

   _____

7. In verse 8, which word means *proud* and *scornful*?

   _____

8. In verse 10, which word means *face*?

   _____

9. In verse 10, which word means *noisy uproar*?

   _____

10. In verse 10, which word means *commanded*?

   _____

FIGURATIVE LANGUAGE

Notice the **boldface** word or phrase in each line from the poem.
Circle a letter to show its meaning.

1. *And then when Cooney* **died** *at first, and Barrows did the same,*

   a. became deathly ill

   b. was put out

   c. took three strikes

   d. heart stopped beating

2. *And Blake, the much despised,* **tore the cover off the ball***;*

   a. peeled off layers

   b. accidentally ripped it

   c. hit it very hard and far

   d. removed the packaging

3. *There was Jimmy safe at second and Flynn* **a-hugging** *third.*

   a. embracing

   b. picking up

   c. grabbing

   d. staying close to

4. *Five thousand tongues* **applauded** *when he wiped them on his shirt.*

   a. cheered

   b. stuck out

   c. clapped

   d. jeered

PUZZLER

Use the clues to help you complete the crossword puzzle.

ACROSS

4. the points or runs made by each team in a game

5. official who calls strikes, balls, and outs

6. the town where Casey played baseball

8. number of players on a baseball team

DOWN

1. insulting word yelled at the umpire when Casey's second strike was called

2. Casey's sport

3. what Mudville had none of

7. one-ninth of a ball game

SYLLABLES

First, write the number of syllables (separate sounds) in each word from the poem. Then rewrite the word, using slashes to separate the syllables. The first one has been done for you.

1. silence

   (2) _si/lence_

2. mountain

   (__) _____

3. eternal

   (__) _____

4. grandeur

   (__) _____

5. sphere

   (__) _____

6. violence

   (__) _____

RHYME SCHEME

PAUL REVERE'S RIDE

1   Listen, my children, and
    you shall hear
Of the midnight ride of
    Paul Revere,
On the eighteenth of April,
    in Seventy-five;
Hardly a man is now alive
Who remembers that famous
    day and year.

2   He said to his friend, "If the
    British march
By land or sea from the town
    to-night,
Hang a lantern aloft in the
    belfry-arch
Of the North Church tower
    as a signal light,—
One, if by land, and two, if by sea;
And I on the opposite shore
    will be,
Ready to ride and spread
    the alarm
Through every Middlesex
    village and farm,
For the country folk to be
    up and to arm."

3   Then he said, "Good night!"
    and with muffled oar
Silently rowed to the
    Charlestown shore,
Just as the moon rose over
    the bay,

Where swinging wide at her
    moorings lay
The *Somerset*, British man-of-war;
A phantom ship, with each
    mast and spar
Across the moon like a prison bar,
And a huge black hulk, that was
    magnified
By its own reflection in the tide.

7   Meanwhile, impatient to mount
    and ride,
Booted and spurred, with a
    heavy stride
On the opposite shore walked
    Paul Revere.
Now he patted his horse's side,
Now gazed at the landscape far
    and near,
Then, impetuous, stamped the earth,
And turned and tightened his
    saddle-girth;
But mostly he watched with eager
    search
The belfry-tower of the Old
    North Church,
As it rose above the graves on the hill,
Lonely and spectral and sombre
    and still.
And lo! as he looks, on the belfry's
    height
A glimmer, and then a gleam of light!
He springs to the saddle, the bridle
    he turns,

But lingers and gazes, till full on
  his sight,
A second lamp in the belfry burns!
A hurry of hoofs in a village street,
A shape in the moonlight, a bulk
  in the dark,
And beneath, from the pebbles,
  in passing, a spark
Struck out by a steed flying
  fearless and fleet:
That was all! And yet, through
  the gloom and the light,
The fate of a nation was riding
  that night;
And the spark struck out by
  that steed, in his flight,
Kindled the land into flame
  with its heat.

9 It was twelve by the village clock,
  When he crossed the bridge into
    Medford town.
  He heard the crowing of the cock,
  And the barking of the farmer's
    dog,
  And felt the damp of the river fog,
  That rises after the sun goes down.

10 It was one by the village clock,
  When he galloped into Lexington.
  He saw the gilded weathercock
  Swim in the moonlight as he passed,
  And the meeting-house windows,
    blank and bare,
  Gaze at him with a spectral glare,
  As if they already stood aghast
  At the bloody work they would
    look upon.

11 It was two by the village clock,
  When he came to the bridge in
    Concord town
  He heard the bleating of the flock,
  And the twitter of birds among
    the trees,
  And he felt the breath of the
    morning breeze

Blowing over the meadows brown.
And one was safe and asleep in
  his bed
Who at the bridge would be first
  to fall,
Who that day would by lying dead,
Pierced by a British musket-ball.

12 You know the rest. In the books
    you have read,
  How the British Regulars fired
    and fled,—
  How the farmers gave them ball
    for ball,
  From behind each fence and
    farm-yard wall,
  Chasing the red-coats down
    the lane,
  Then crossing the fields to
    emerge again
  Under the trees at the turn of
    the road
  And only pausing to fire and load.

13 So through the night rode Paul
    Revere;
  And so through the night went
    his cry of alarm
  To every Middlesex village and
    farm,—
  A cry of defiance and not of fear,
  A voice in the darkness, a knock
    at the door,
  And a word that shall echo
    forevermore!
  For, borne on the night-wind
    of the Past,
  Through all our history, to the last,
  In the hour of darkness and peril
    and need,
  The people will waken and listen
    to hear
  The hurrying hoof-beats of that
    steed
  And the midnight message of
    Paul Revere.

COMPREHENSION

Answer the questions in complete sentences.

1. How was Revere's friend supposed to signal him when the British troops started to move? _____

_____

2. What was the signal if the British were coming by land? By sea?

_____

_____

3. How did Revere get to the opposite side of the river? _____

_____

4. Why was it important for Revere to spread the alarm?

_____

_____

_____

5. In what way can Paul Revere's ride be considered a success?

_____

_____

6. According to the author, what will people in the future hear during times of trouble? _____

_____

SEQUENCE OF EVENTS

Number the events in the poem to show which happened first, second, and so on.

_____ Paul Revere came to the bridge in Concord town.

_____ Paul Revere saw two lamps in the belfry tower.

_____ Paul Revere rowed to the Charlestown shore.

_____ Paul Revere galloped into Lexington.

_____ The farmers chased the redcoats down the lane.

_____ Paul Revere asked his friend to hang a lantern in the belfry tower.

_____ Paul Revere watched the belfry tower for the signal.

_____ Paul Revere crossed the bridge into Medford town.

VOCABULARY

Find the following words in the poem. Then use context clues to help you figure out what each word means. Finally, write the meanings on the lines. Use a dictionary if you need help.

1. **moorings** _____

2. **hulk** _____

3. **impetuous** _____

4. **girth** _____

5. **spectral** _____

RHYMING

First read the **boldface** words from verse 11 of the poem. Then write the words with the same sounds at the ends of the other lines in verse 11. Finally, write two of your own words that rhyme with the words from the poem. The first one has been done for you.

1. **clock** _____*flock*_____ _____*rock*_____ _____*dock*_____

2. **town** _____ _____ _____

3. **trees** _____ _____ _____

4. **bed** _____ _____ _____

5. **fall** _____ _____ _____

IDENTIFYING RHYTHM

Rhythm is the pattern of accented and unaccented syllables in a poem. In "Paul Revere's Ride," each line of verse has four accented syllables. For example, read the first line of the poem aloud. Emphasize each underlined syllable:

<u>Lis</u>/ten, my <u>chil</u>/dren, and <u>you</u> shall <u>hear</u>

Now read aloud the nine lines of verse 2. Underline the four accented syllables in each line.

1. He said to his friend, "If the Brit/ish march

2. By land or sea from the town to/night,

3. Hang a lan/tern a/loft in the bel/fry arch

4. Of the North Church tow/er as a sig/nal light,—

5. One, if by land, and two, if by sea;

6. And I on the op/po/site shore will be,

7. Read/y to ride and spread the a/larm

8. Through ev/ery Mid/dle/sex vil/lage and farm,

9. For the coun/try folk to be up and to arm."

PUZZLER

First, unscramble the names from the poem. Then use the unscrambled names to correctly complete the sentences below.

CRONDOC   DROMFED   LOWTHENSCAR

_____   _____   _____

DEXILMEDS   MOSEREST   GLONIXNET

_____   _____   _____

1. Revere galloped into _____ at one o'clock.

2. The _____ looked like a phantom ship.

3. At twelve o'clock, Revere crossed the bridge into _____.

4. Revere silently rowed to the _____ shore.

5. His cry of alarm went to every _____ village and farm.

6. At two o'clock, Revere came to the bridge in _____.

POINT OF VIEW

Before reading . . .

"The Rime of the Ancient Mariner" is a long narrative poem written by the English poet Samuel Taylor Coleridge. This lesson presents the second part of the poem. As you read, notice that it is written in the first person—from the ancient mariner's point of view.

THE RIME OF THE ANCIENT MARINER
(Part 2)

1   "The sun now rose upon the right:
     Out of the sea came he,
     Still hid in mist, and on the left
     Went down into the sea.

2   And the good south wind still blew behind,
     But no sweet bird did follow,
     Nor any day for food or play
     Came to the mariners' hollo!

3   And I had done a hellish thing,
     And it would work 'em woe:
     For all averred, I had killed the bird
     That made the breeze to blow.
     "Ah wretch!" said they, "the bird to slay,
     That made the breeze to blow!"

4   Nor dim nor red, like God's own head,
     The glorious Sun uprist:
     Then all averred, I had killed the bird
     That brought the fog and mist.
     "'Twas right," said they, "such birds to slay,
     That bring the fog and mist."

5   The fair breeze blew, the white foam flew,
     The furrow followed free;
     We were the first that ever burst
     Into that silent sea.

6   Down dropt the breeze, the sails dropt down,
     'Twas sad as sad could be;
     And we did speak only to break
     The silence of the sea!

7   All in a hot and copper sky,
     The bloody Sun, at noon,
     Right up above the mast did stand,
     No bigger than the Moon.

8   Day after day, day after day,
     We stuck, nor breath nor motion;
     As idle as a painted ship
     Upon a painted ocean.

9   Water, water, everywhere,
     And all the boards did shrink;
     Water, water, everywhere
     Nor any drop to drink.

10   The very deep did rot: O Christ!
     That ever this should be!
     Yea, slimy things did crawl with legs
     Upon the slimy sea.

11   About, about, in reel and rout
     The death-fires danced at night;
     The water, like a witch's oils,
     Burnt green, and blue, and white.

12   And some in dreams assured were
     Of the Spirit that plagued us so;
     Nine fathom deep he had followed us
     From the land of mist and snow.

13   And every tongue, through utter drought,
     Was withered at the root;
     We could not speak, no more than if
     We had been choked with soot.

14   Ah! well-a-day! what evil looks
     Had I from old and young!
     Instead of the cross, the Albatross
     About my neck was hung.

COMPREHENSION

Answer the questions in complete sentences.

1. What was the "hellish thing" that the ancient mariner had done?

   _____

2. What kind of bird no longer came by when the sailors cried "hollo"?

   _____

3. Why were the sailors at first upset when they no longer saw

   the bird? _____

   _____

4. Why did the sailors later change their minds and approve of

   the fact that the bird was gone? _____

   _____

5. What problems did the sailors face once the breeze died down?

   _____

6. According to the ancient mariner, there was water everywhere.

   Why were the sailors faced with a problem regarding water?

   _____

   _____

7. What spirit did some sailors dream was following the ship?

   _____

8. What did the ancient mariner mean when he said that the

   albatross was hung about his neck? _____

   _____

IDENTIFYING RHYTHM

Rhythm is the pattern of accented (emphasized) and unaccented syllables in a poem. In "The Rime of the Ancient Mariner," each line of verse has either three or four accented syllables. For example, read aloud the first line of the poem. Emphasize the underlined syllables.

"The <u>sun</u> now <u>rose</u> up/<u>on</u> the <u>right</u>:

Now read aloud the following lines. Note the *accented* syllables in each line.

Verse 1 <u>Out</u> of the <u>sea</u> came <u>he</u>,

     Still <u>hid</u> in <u>mist</u>, and <u>on</u> the <u>left</u>

     Went <u>down</u> in/<u>to</u> the <u>sea</u>.

Verse 2 And the <u>good</u> south <u>wind</u> still <u>blew</u> be/<u>hind</u>,

     But <u>no</u> sweet <u>bird</u> did <u>fol</u>/low,

     Nor <u>an</u>/y day for <u>food</u> or <u>play</u>

     <u>Came</u> to the <u>mar</u>/i/ners' <u>hol</u>/lo!

IDENTIFYING REPETITION AND ALLITERATION

Repetition in a poem is the repeated use of any element of language—a sound, word, phrase, entire line, or group of lines. *Alliteration* is the repetition of the same sound at the beginning of two or more words (example: *soft silent snowflakes).* Answer the following questions on the lines.

1. Which line in verse 3 is a repetition of line 4? _____

2. In verse 3, line 2, which words are an example of alliteration? _____

3. In verse 6, line 1, which words are an example of alliteration?

   _____

4. Which lines in verse 9 are an example of repetition? _____

5. In verse 5, line 2, the words *furrow followed free* are an example of _____.

VOCABULARY

Find the **boldface** words below in the poem. Use context clues to figure out the meaning of each word. Then put a checkmark (✔) next to the correct definition.

1. **mariners**

   _____ deep sea marine life

   _____ sailors

   _____ certain kinds of seafood

   _____ sailing ships

3. **furrow**

   _____ a groove or trench

   _____ the skin of certain animals

   _____ a warm winter coat

   _____ furnishing

2. **averred**

   _____ averaged

   _____ turned toward

   _____ avenged

   _____ verified

4. **plagued**

   _____ stole

   _____ pledged

   _____ annoyed or disturbed

   _____ stricken with a serious illness

IDENTIFYING RHYME

Look back at the poem to answer these questions about rhyming words. Write your answers on the lines.

1. Which word in verse 1, line 2, rhymes with the word at the end of the line? _____

2. In verse 2, which two words at the ends of lines rhyme? _____

3. In verse 5, line 3, which word within the line rhymes with the word at the end of the line? _____

4. Which word in verse 5, line 2, rhymes with the word *swallowed?* _____

5. Which word in verse 7, line 3, rhymes
   with the word *band*? _____

6. In verse 8, which two words
   at the ends of lines rhyme? _____

PUZZLER

Unscramble the words from the poem. Then use the words to complete the
sentences. Finally, rearrange the circled letters to complete the last sentence.

PR(O)D	TH(O)DRUG	TU(C)(K)(S)
_____	_____	_____
BAL(S)OT(R)AS	ZE(B)ERE	D(W)IN
_____	_____	_____

1. The sailors suffered from the effects of the _____.

2. When the _____ dropped, the sails dropped.

3. At first, a good south _____ blew.

4. The _____ made the breeze blow.

5. There was water everywhere, but not a _____
   to drink.

6. The ship got _____ when the wind died.

   The ancient mariner used a __ __ __ __ __ __ __ __
   to kill the albatross.

REPETITION

Before reading . . .

"The Charge of the Light Brigade" was written by the English poet Alfred, Lord Tennyson. The story told in this poem was inspired by actual news reports of the day. The poem honors the bravery of the British troops at the Battle of Balaklava during the Crimean War in 1854. As you read, notice how the poet uses repetition to create a musical quality.

THE CHARGE OF THE LIGHT BRIGADE

1 Half a league, half a league,
Half a league onward,
All in the valley of Death
   Rode the six hundred.
"Forward the Light Brigade!
Charge for the guns!" he said:
Into the valley of Death
   Rode the six hundred.

2 "Forward the Light Brigade!"
Was there a man dismay'd?
Not tho' the soldier knew
   Someone had blunder'd:
Theirs not to make reply
Theirs not to reason why,
Theirs but to do and die:
Into the valley of Death
   Rode the six hundred.

3 Cannon to right of them,
Cannon to left of them,
Cannon in front of them
   Volley'd and thunder'd:
Storm'd at with shot and shell,
Boldly they rode and well,
Into the jaws of Death,
Into the mouth of Hell
   Rode the six hundred.

4 Flash'd all their sabres bare,
     Flash'd as they turn'd in air
     Sabring the gunners there,
     Charging an army, while
       All the world wonder'd:
     Plunged in the battery-smoke
     Right thro' the line they broke;
     Cossack and Russian
     Reel'd from the sabre-stroke
     Shatter'd and sunder'd.
     Then they rode back, but not
       Not the six hundred.

5 Cannon to right of them,
     Cannon to left of them,
     Cannon behind them
       Volley'd and thunder'd;
     Storm'd at with shot and shell,
     While horse and hero fell,
     They that had fought so well
     Came thro' the jaws of Death
     Back from the mouth of Hell,
     All that was left of them,
       Left of six hundred.

6 When can their glory fade?
     O the wild charge they made!
       All the world wonder'd.
     Honor the charge they made!
     Honor the Light Brigade,
       Noble six hundred!

COMPREHENSION

Answer the questions in complete sentences.

1. Why do you think the poet referred to the battleground as

   the "valley of Death"? _____

_____

2. What is the poet's opinion of the command ordering the British

  troops to charge? _____

  _____

3. What is the poet's opinion of the troops of the Light Brigade and

  the way they carried out their command? _____

  _____

4. How does the poet wish the rest of the world to respond to the

  charge of the Light Brigade? _____

  _____

5. According to the poet, how should a soldier respond to orders?

  _____

IDENTIFYING CONTRACTIONS

The poet has removed one or more letters from several words in the poem, replacing them with an apostrophe. This is an old-fashioned, poetic way of writing a *contraction*. Identify 10 of these contractions in the poem and write them on the lines. Next to each contraction, replace the apostrophe with the missing letter or letters. The first one has been done for you.

dismay'd   _dismayed_   _____   _____

_____   _____   _____   _____

_____   _____   _____   _____

_____   _____   _____   _____

IDENTIFYING REPETITION

Repetition in a poem is the repeated use of any element of language—a sound, word, phrase, entire line, or group of lines. The following questions refer to the use of repetition in "The Charge of the Light Brigade." Write your answers on the lines.

1. The poet ends each verse either with "Rode the six hundred"
   or a different line that also includes the words "six hundred."
   Write the other lines that include "six hundred."

   _____

   _____

   _____

2. Write the lines from verse 3 that are repeated in verse 5.

   _____

   _____

   _____

   _____

IDENTIFYING RHYME

Look back at the poem to answer these questions about rhyming words.
Write your answers on the lines.

1. Which word in verse 2 rhymes with *Brigade?* _____

2. List four words in the poem that rhyme with the word *hundred.*

   _____   _____

   _____   _____

3. List the words in verse 4 that rhyme with the word *smoke.*

_____

4. List the words in verse 5 that rhyme with the word *shell.*

_____

5. List four words of your own that rhyme with the word *light.*

_____ _____

_____ _____

IDENTIFYING ALLITERATION

Alliteration is the repetition of the same sound at the beginning of words (example: *soft silent snowflakes*). Check the correct answer to each question.

1. Which of the following lines from verse 3 contains an example of alliteration?

    _____ Boldly they rode and well,

    _____ Cannon to the left of them,

    _____ Storm'd at with shot and shell,

    _____ Volley'd and thunder'd:

2. Which of the following lines from verse 4 contains an example of alliteration?

    _____ Flash'd all their sabres bare,

    _____ Right thro' the line they broke;

    _____ Plunged in the battery-smoke

    _____ All the world wonder'd:

NOTING DETAILS

Write answers to the following questions on the lines.

1. The poet refers to the "valley of Death" in what two other ways?

   _____   _____

2. Who were the British troops fighting against? _____

   _____

3. What happened to the enemy when the British charged?

   _____

4. What was the exact wording of the command ordering the

   British troops into the "valley of Death"? _____

   _____

PUZZLER

Use the clues to help you solve the crossword puzzle.
Answers are words from the poem.

ACROSS

1. large gun mounted on a base
3. army unit made up of two or
   more battalions
6. a country's soldiers, trained for war
7. old-fashioned measure of distance;
   about three miles

DOWN

1. to rush at with force; to attack
2. The six hundred rode into
   the "mouth" of this.
4. great honor or fame
5. slowly disappear

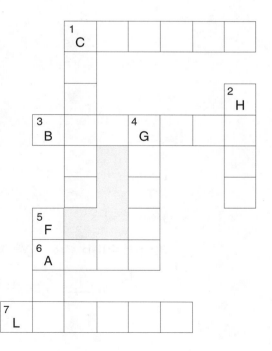

REVIEW

RECALLING DETAILS OF PLOT

The plot, or sequence of actions, is just as important in a narrative poem as in a novel or short story. Circle the letter next to the correct answer for each of the following questions.

1. As Casey haughtily ignored the first two pitches, how did the audience respond each time when the umpire called "strike"?

   a. They enthusiastically applauded.

   b. They booed and shouted angry words at the umpire.

2. How did Paul Revere ask his friend to signal him regarding British troop movements?

   a. Two if by land, one if by sea.

   b. One if by land, two if by sea.

3. What was the *effect* of Paul Revere's midnight ride?

   a. The British won a decisive victory against the Americans.

   b. The Americans were able to fight off the British.

4. What did the ancient mariner do that resulted in severe problems for the crew on his ship?

   a. He established a friendly relationship with an albatross.

   b. He killed an albatross that had been following the ship.

5. Why did the soldiers of the Light Brigade charge into the valley of Death?

   a. They didn't think it would be very dangerous.

   b. They had been trained to never question a command.

GLOSSARY OF READING TERMS

adapted rewritten to be made shorter or easier to read

alliteration repetition of the initial sound in two or more words; a poetic device

analyze to identify and examine the separate parts of a whole

author's purpose the writer's specific goal or reason for writing a particular book, article, etc.

categorize to divide into main subjects or groups

cause a happening or situation that makes something else happen as a result

classify to organize according to some similarity

compare to make note of how two or more things are alike

compound word a word made by combining two or more smaller words

conclusion the end or last part of a novel, article, etc.

context clues the words in a sentence just before and after an unfamiliar word or phrase. Context clues help to make clear what the unfamiliar word means.

contrast to make note of how two or more things are different from one another

describe to tell or write about something or someone in detail in order to help the reader or listener create a mental image

details bits of information or description that support the main idea and make it clearer

dialogue lines spoken by characters in a story or play

discuss to talk or write about a topic, giving various opinions and ideas

effect the reaction or impact that occurs as a result of a cause

elements the essential parts or components of a whole

excerpt section quoted from a book, article, etc.

fact something that actually happened or is really true

fiction literary work in which the plot and characters are imagined by the author

figurative language colorful, nonliteral use of words and phrases to achieve a dramatic effect

generalize to form a general rule or idea after considering particular facts

graphs charts or diagrams that visually present changes in something or the relationship between two or more changing things

homonyms words pronounced alike but having different meanings and usually different spellings

identify to name or point out; to distinguish someone or something from others

image idea, impression; a picture in the mind

inference conclusion arrived at by careful reasoning

interpret to explain the meaning of; to figure out in one's own way

judgment a decision made after weighing various facts

literature the entire body of written work including fiction, nonfiction, drama, poetry, etc.

locate find; tell where something is

main idea the point or central thought in a written work or part of a work

multiple-meaning words lookalike words that have different meanings in different contexts

nonfiction writing about the real world, real people, actual events, etc.

objective reflecting what is actual or real; expressed without bias or opinion

order items arranged or sequenced in a certain way, such as alphabetical order or order of importance

organize to put in place according to a system

outcome the result; the way that something turns out

parts of speech grammatical classifications of eight word types: adjective, adverb, conjunction, interjection, noun, preposition, pronoun, or verb

passage section of a written work

plot the chain of events in a story that leads to the story's outcome

plural word form showing more than one person, place, or thing

point of view the position from which something is observed or told; when a character tells the story, *first person* point of view is used; an author who tells the story in his own voice is using *third person* point of view.

predict to foretell what you think will happen in the future

prefix group of letters added at the beginning of a word to change the word's meaning or function

recall to remember or bring back to mind

refer to speak of something or call attention to it

relationship a connection of some kind between two or more persons, things, events, etc.

scan to glance at something or look over it quickly

sequence items in order; succession; one thing following another

singular word form naming just one person, place, or thing

subjective reflecting personal ideas, opinions, or experiences

suffix group of letters added at the end of a word that changes the word's meaning or function

symbol a concrete object used to represent an abstract idea

table an orderly, graphic arrangement of facts, figures, etc.

tense verb form that shows the time of the action, such as past, present, or future

term word or phrase with a special meaning in a certain field of study such as art, history, etc.

tone the feeling given by the author's choice of language

vocabulary all the words of a language